RECIPES
from
SWEET YESTERDAY
by
Thelma Allen

To Sharron —
cooking is fun!
Thelma

RECIPES FROM SWEET YESTERDAY – Volume Two
Thelma Allen

Second printing, January 1998
Third printing, May 2000

Published by:
Sweet Yesterday
P. O. Box 111510
Nashville, TN 37222

Author: Thelma Allen
Editors: Thelma Allen and Michael Allen
Graphic design/layout: Michael Allen
Illustrations: Sylvia Worcester
Cover photography: Michael Allen
Cover photograph models: Thelma Allen and her
          grandson, Allen Worcester
Kitchen in cover photograph furnished by Ilena
          Vernon
Electronic Prepress: McPherson and Kelley, Inc.
Printing: Harris Press, Inc.

ISBN 0966832-1-3

TABLE OF CONTENTS

DEDICATION

It's only natural that I would dedicate this book to my sister, Marie Rogers Mills. I can't remember when there wasn't a Marie in my life; since, I'm only 15 months older than her. There has never been a time in our lives that we couldn't see one another every day or at least have a telephone conversation. We've seen lots of changes in the telecommunication system. At first we turned a crank to get an operator that said, "Number Please." Marie was always there for me.

We did everything together. Due to convenience and birthdays we started and finished school together. We studied together and did our work together. We laughed together and cried together. Yes, we fought together, but very rarely. It would break my heart, if I thought I hurt her feelings. I hate to think what it would have been like without her. We had to stick together to survive the loss of our mother and then the problems of *The Great Depression*. Our mother taught us to do so many things. It seemed as though she realized she had such a short time to fortify us for life.

Without knowing it, as I look back now, we were really organized. We took turns doing our work. If I was making up the beds, Marie would cook breakfast; then next week we switched jobs. Both of us did the dishes. If I washed the dishes, she would dry them. The one that dried them also swept the kitchen, while the other washed the pots and pans. If my mother needed a spool of thread, we'd saddle "Old Roan" and go 3 miles to the little store. If Marie road in the saddle going, then I would ride outside the saddle. Then I'd get to ride inside the saddle coming back; she'd ride on the outside.

We were even organized when we wanted to do something that we weren't sure we were to permitted to do. Marie would do the asking, and I would cry. I could cry easier than she. It didn't work everytime.

Marie married a farmer. They worked really hard and were very successful. Her husband, Jack, died suddenly in 1974 from a heart attack. They raised 2 boys, Bob and Joe. Marie still manages the farm business with the help of 1 son. The other son teaches school some distance away.

Thanks, Marie, for being everything you'd want in a sister.

Marie Mills

INTRODUCTION

My purpose for writing this book is still the same as my first cookbook - to pass on to posterity the customs and habits that made up the lifestyles of the pioneers, their farm life of work and play, especially the early years of my parents. I never thought the world owed me a living. I hope I can always be on the tax roll, not the welfare roll. The cookbooks are helping me stay on the tax roll.

When I started my first cookbook, I never dreamed there would be a second. I just couldn't do all I wanted in 1 book. In this book, I'm still not doing all I want to do. Consequently, there will need to be number three, if God will grant me the time.

When I started the first book, I wondered if I would have enough recipes. I'm often asked how do I come up with so many recipes. That's no problem. My old friends and my newly-acquired friends have generously supplied me with wonderful recipes that are tried and true for which I'm very grateful.

Other than my early training by my mother, Mrs. Mills, my sister's mother-in-law, inspired and taught me more about the art of cooking than anybody. She was such a delightful person who loved to cook and entertain, especially at the dinner table. I'm sure this book is better because of her.

Mrs. Mills was born in 1867. She received a B. S. degree from Commerce State Teachers College in 1898, as it was called then. She, in that era, was the only person I knew that collected and cooked with recipes. She attended every cooking school in her area, and she loved to try new recipes.

Mrs. Mills and her husband, Joe, both were school teachers. They married at the age of 35. She was 40 years old when her only child, Jack, was born. She taught until Jack would have been her student. She never wanted to teach her own son, so she retired.

She often cooked Sunday and holiday dinners for Marie and Jack, my brother Charlie and his wife, and Marvin and me. She wouldn't let anybody help with the dishes. She wanted to visit and do the dishes when her guests were gone. Her dining room was furnished with lovely furniture and the best dishes and silver she could afford. There was always a linen tablecloth and cloth napkins. The rest of her house was very ordinary.

They always milked a cow, so she could have all the fresh cream, butter and buttermilk that she loved to cook with. After her husband died, she still milked the cow. Marie and I made dresses, curtains and even boxer shorts for the men from her feed sacks, especially during the *Depression Days* and *World War II*. She always had a cookie jar, a gallon crock with a lid, that was never empty. People would drive out from town to buy her fresh eggs and cream. They knew where the cookie jar was.

Mrs. Mills was an avid reader and often read to Jack and Joe in the evenings by a coal oil lamp. Rural electrication didn't come until the Roosevelt era and *World War II*. She always had a daily newspaper and *The Saturday Evening Post*.

She was no doubt the wittiest person I have ever known. Here are just a few of her witty quotes:

In describing someone that looked kind of "bedraggled," she would say, "They look like the tail end of pea time."

The dresses in the '30s and '40s had rhinestone belt buckles. She would never wear the buckle. She said, "Those buckles remind me of a lightning rod on a hog house." It was always understood that she would buy a new outfit, dress shoes and a hat every Spring and Fall.

When she was 70 years old, she was asked why didn't she learn to drive. Her reply was, "I already know how to do enough things."

Mrs. Mills said, "God knew what He was doing when He didn't let old women have babies." She also said, "If there was a Heaven on earth, God wouldn't have needed to make a Heaven."

My thanks to Mrs. Mills.

Thanks to all the people who gave me recipes. I know you will enjoy the recipes, pioneer history, philosophy, and helpful information in the cookbook. I have enjoyed doing it for you.

Thelma Allen

This photograph of Thelma
was made when she was nine months old in Perrin, Texas.

PORK

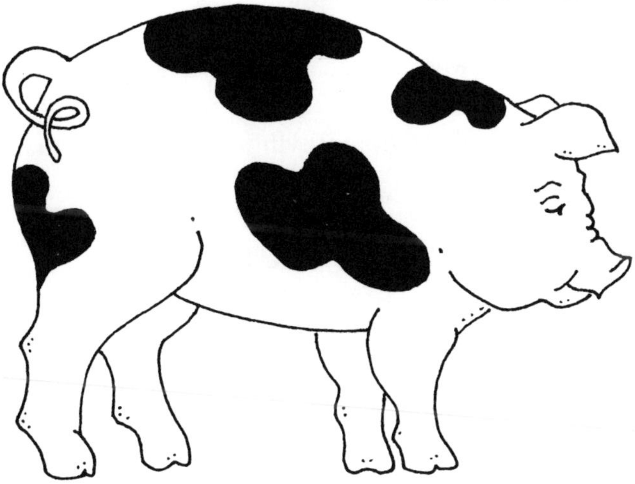

HOG KILLING DAYS

In my first book, I gave you the information on hog killing days; how we prepared all we could the day before in readiness for the eventful day. It was eventful - lots of activity and lots of good food.

Now, I'm bringing you a method a few years later that replaced the first method. It was much easier, but it was still hard work and just as eventful.

This next story was written by my friend, Ruth Edens of Ponca City, Oklahoma. She tells about the hog killing days when she was still at home living with her parents, Ernie and Stella Baugham.

THE DAY WE BUTCHERED

"Butchering was always done on a very cool day in early Winter. My father used a block and tackle to pull the hog up by its hind legs after they stuck it to bleed. It was then scraped of all hair and cleaned. After it was skinned, the hams and shoulders were cut off.

"The best part of the day was when the fluffy crisp cracklin's came out of the oven. They were allowed to cool and then were salted. Mother always chose the skins that were free of hair stubs. They smelled and tasted so good.

"The feet were cleaned for pickling. The hams and shoulders were taken to the ice plant for curing and then placed in the frozen food locker. The pork chops, steaks and roasts were also placed in the locker along with the Spring calf that had been butchered.

"The ribs were always cooked the same day; sometimes with homemade sauerkraut or just with spices. The neck bones were cooked, and the broth and bits of meat from them were combined with cornmeal and placed in the icebox to cool. It was then sliced, dredged in flour, and fried for breakfast the next morning. The flour helped it to brown and hold it together.

"The meat scraps were ground into sausage. It had spices added. Then patties were fried and placed in jars. The rendering was poured over them piping hot, and they were cover with lids. They did not have to be sealed, because the lard poured over them acted as a sealer. When mother was ready to serve them for breakfast on a future day, all she had to do was put them in the oven in a pan with a rack until all the fat drained off. They were crisp and very delicious.

"All the rendering that was left was placed in a large bucket to cook with while fresh and then later made into lye soap. It was wonderful to wash with, and the white clothes were always so white.

"This was the time when our country was coming out of The Depression. We were so poor but never hungry. There was always wild berries to be picked, nuts of all descriptions to be gathered, a cow that furnished us with plenly milk, home-made butter and cottage cheese, and beef. There were greens in the Spring served with cornbread and buttermilk. That made a perfect meal.

"Always thinking ahead, my wonderful parents fed a family of seven, 3 wonderful meals a day. Thank you, Mom and Dad."

Ruth Baugham Edens

HOG HEAD CHEESE
Ruth Edens

Scrape and clean head. Remove short hairs and tongue. Remove all the undesirable parts. Place tongue and head in a large pot of slightly salted water. Simmer until meat falls from the bones.

Drain and strain liquids and set aside. Chop 3 red pepper and 1 large onion very fine. Run meat through a course blade of the food grinder. Mix peppers, onions and meat. Add black pepper and sage to taste, if desired. Add 2 tsp. + 1 cup of vinegar. Press into loaf pans; pour ½ cup liquid over each loaf. Allow to cool; preferable in icebox overnight. Slice and serve as sandwich meat.

SAUSE
Ruth Edens

Wash and scrape pigs feet. Cover with water in a large pot. Boil until the meat falls from the bones. Pick meat from bones, add 2 cups of liquid that the feet have been cooked in. Pour into a loaf after seasoning to taste with salt, black pepper and vinegar. Allow to jell. Broth has a natural gelatin from pigs feet. Slice and serve.

SCRAPPLE
Ruth Edens

Neck bones are broken into pieces and placed in a kettle with enough water to cover them. Cook until meat falls off the bones. For each pint of meat pulled from the bones place 3 pints of boiling liquid from neck bones in kettle along with the pint of meat. In bowl mix 1 pint of cornmeal and 1 pint of water. Stir this in a kettle and let boil. Stir with large wooden spoon, as this will pop and splatter. After it thickens, pour into 2 loaf pans. Chill overnight. After cooled and firm, slice and dredge in flour. Place in skillet of hot grease (lard). Flour will help it brown and hold its shape. Good with scrambled eggs for breakfast or with butter beans for an evening meal.

LYE SOAP
FOR ALL NEEDS
given to me by Irma Bryce
in memory of her mother

Render all fats (hogs or beef). Clean rancid fats by boiling in a volume of water. Chill by adding 1 quart of cold water to each gallon of liquid. Remove fat from top. Add 1 can of lye and 2 ½ pints of soft, cold water. Stir until spoon can stand on its own. When all the lye is incorporated into fat, pour into a cardboard or lined wooden box. Let stand 24 hours. Remove and cut into bars. Keep dry in room temperature for 2 weeks to cure.

CRACKLIN' BREAD

2 cups cracklin' (made from
        rendering lard)
1 tsp. salt
2 cups cornmeal
hot water

Cube cracklin' in small pieces and pour salt over them. Add enough hot water to make a stiff paste. Divide into oblong loaves and bake at 400° for 30 minutes.

My mother never made pickled pigs feet. I know she never threw away anything. They must have gone into the mincemeat.

PICKLED PIG'S FEET

4 pig's feet
2 tsp. whole cloves
1 bay leaf
4 cups vinegar
1 Tbsp. salt
1 onion
½ tsp. pepper

Wash and scrape pig's feet. Boil until meat slips from bone. Drain. Place meat in bowl. Combine vinegar, cloves, salt, pepper, bay leaf, and onion. Boil 30 minutes. Add 2 cups of broth in which the pig's feet were cooked. Strain. Pour over pigs feet. Let stand for 3 days before using.

HAM BAKED IN MILK

Cut from the center of a well-cured ham a slice 2 or 3 inches thick. Soak for 2 hours in cold water and wipe dry. Put in a casserole dish that has been well-greased with butter. Sprinkle with a little brown sugar and cover with sweet milk. Cook in a 300° oven until tender.

WHY NOT BUY A WHOLE HAM?

Have the shank end cut away; then cut in half lengthwise. Then cut from the bone portion. Cut out pieces of meat to grind for patties or casseroles. You can make patties (freeze or refrigerate) for breakfast. The bone is really good to cook with vegetables like cabbage or beans. Try black-eye peas for a change. The butt end is now left, also the other portion of the shank. You can grind meat from the shank for ham loaf. You can get 2 thick slices from the butt end. They can be broiled or fried. The remaining part can be baked.

HAM WITH TURNIPS

1½ lbs. ham (cut 1" thick)
6 cloves
nutmeg
½ cup honey
2 cups sliced cooked turnips
¼ cup water

Place ham in baking pan. Stick cloves in ham. Sprinkle with nutmeg. Add water and honey. Cover. Bake in slow oven at 325° for about 45 minutes or until meat is tender. Remove from oven. Cover ham with turnips. Return to oven. Bake until brown. If desired, sweet potatoes may be used instead of parships. To me it is so delicious with sweet potatoes. Serves 6.

Ham seems to be a favorite of just about everyone, but country ham is strickly Southern. Most Southern cooks have their special way of preparing it. This is my favorite. My folks cured our hams, and they were cooked outside in the black iron wash kettle.

COUNTRY HAM

1 country ham
2 cups dark molasses
1 cup vinegar
whole cloves
brown sugar
pickle juice

Place ham in a large kettle. Cover with cold water. Add 1 cup molasses and 1 cup vinegar. Let stand overnight. Remove ham from water, rinse well and cover with fresh water. Add remaining molasses. Cover. Bring to a rolling boil over high heat. Boil for 30 minutes. Remove kettle from heat. Do not remove cover. Let stand overnight. Remove ham from water. Remove rind. Score; stud with cloves. Combine brown sugar and pickle juice to make paste. Spread over ham. Bake at 350° for 30 minutes. I like to use canned peach or apricot juice.

BAKED HAM
VIRGINIA STYLE

Use 1 ham about 12 lbs. Scrub really well with small brush and scrape off any mold. Put in large size kettle with enough cold water to cover. Put 1 small bay leaf, 1 sliced onion, 2 or 3 stalks of celery, 2 sprigs of parsley, optional. Bring water to boiling point and simmer slowly for about 4 hours. When time is up, lift the ham from the broth, put it down on a firm surface and peel off the top skin, leaving a little around the shank end. Then put the ham in a baking pan, fat side up, together with a cup of ham broth and 1 cup of cider. Put in moderate oven for 1 hour and baste every 10 minutes or so. When it is finished, score the fat surface evenly and spread it with brown sugar and bread crumbs. Dot it with cloves and put back in the oven for browning. Do not baste while browning.

No Virginian will forgive you if you forget the cider sauce - which is as follows: Put 1 cup of ham liquid into the pan where the ham was baked. Cream butter and flour for thickening purposes and bring sauce to boil. Then add 1/3 cup of cider. Season the sauce with a few grains of paprika and be sure to strain it before you serve it.

MRS. MILLS'
SWEET AND SOUR SPARERIBS

3 lbs. ribs
1 medium onion (chopped)
2 Tbsp. butter
2 Tbsp. flour
2 Tbsp. brown sugar
3 Tbsp. Worcestershire sauce
1 Tbsp. prepared mustard
½ cup vinegar
½ cup catsup
½ cup celery
1 cup water

Brown ribs. Combine ingredients and pour over ribs. Place in a baking dish and bake in a 350° oven for 1½ hours.

COUNTRY STYLE RIBS

For a change why not take the fat off country style pork ribs. Put in a covered casserole dish. Salt and pepper to taste. Bake in 350° oven until tender. Take the lid off the last 10 minutes. Make some cream gravy, fry some skillet potatoes, open some green beans; season with some of the pork drippings.

Pass the hot biscuits! Serve with tart apples. Just don't eat too much, and you won't feel guilty.

TEXAS BARBECUED SPARERIBS
so - so good!

3 lbs. spareribs
lemon slices
½ onion (chopped)
2 Tbsp. brown sugar
1 tsp. salt
1 tsp. dry mustard
¼ tsp. chili powder
⅛ tsp. cayenne pepper
2 Tbsp. Worcestershire sauce
1 can tomato sauce
¼ cup catsup
½ cup water

Cut spareribs into serving pieces; place in roasting pan. Arrange 1 lemon slice on each serving. Sprinkle with onion. Bake in a 450° oven for 30 minutes. Mix all remaining ingredients in saucepan. Simmer for 15 minutes or until thickened slightly. Pour over ribs; reduce oven temperature to 350°. Bake for 1 hour, basting every 15 minutes with sauce. Add water, if necessary.

MARIE MILLS' GOLDEN CHOPS
different

4 thick pork chops
1 green pepper
2 medium onions
2 Tbsp. pimento
6 crackers
½ cup milk

Brown pork chops in butter. I use part shortening. Place in a baking dish. Grind green pepper, onions, pimento, and crackers together. Season with salt and pepper. Moisten with milk, heap on pork chops and bake at 375° for 45 minutes.

ALMOND-FRIED RICE WITH PORK CHOPS
Juarine Wooldridge

¼ cup butter
1 large onion (chopped)
1 green pepper (chopped)
4 pork chops (smoked)
½ tsp. pepper
salt to taste
¼ cup soy sauce
1 cup toasted almonds (slivered)
4 cups cooked rice
1 Tbsp. chopped pimento
        (optional)

Melt butter in heavy skillet; saute' onion and green pepper until wilted. Add pork, pepper, salt, soy sauce, almonds, and rice. Simmer until pork is done and flavors are blended. Add pimento just before serving.

This recipe makes a pretty platter.

ROAST PORK DINNER

1- 4 lb. roast loin of pork
1½ tsp. salt
½ tsp. caraway seed
⅛ tps. pepper
½ cup chopped fresh onions
butter
2½ lbs. small potatoes

Sprinkle pork with salt, caraway seeds and pepper; place in shallow baking pan. Bake in 325° oven for about an hour. Pour off excess drippings. Saute' onions in butter in a skillet. Add to roast with a small amount of water. Bake for 30 minutes longer. Peel small potatoes and boil in salted water for 8 minutes in a covered saucepan. Drain. Place potatoes around roast. Bake for 1 hour; turning occasionally. Place roast on heated serving platter. Garnish with parsley.

BROILED PORK TENDERLOIN

Select thick tenderloins and have split for broiling. Rub with melted butter and season with salt and pepper and a tiny pinch of sage or poultry seasoning. Broil under a moderate heat until nicely browned. Serve with tart applesauce.

PORK STEAK CASSEROLE

1½ lb. pork steak (cubed)
1 cup celery (chopped)
1 cup onion (chopped)
1 can mushroom pieces
1 can mushroom soup
1 (8 oz.) package wide noodles
    (cooked)
2 Tbsp. butter

Brown steak in small amount fat in skillet. Add celery and onions with ½ cup water. Simmer for 12 minutes or until celery is tender. Add mushrooms and soup. Rinse cans with 1 cup water. Add to mixture. Cook noodles by direction on package. Drain and add to pork mixture. Pour into casserole. Top with butter. Bake at 350° for 45 minutes. Serves 4.

BREADED PORK TENDERLOIN

Have tenderloin cut in crosswise sections and flattened with a cleaver. Dip in fine dry bread crumbs, then in beaten eggs that 2 Tbsp. of water has been added, then again in bread crumbs. Saute' in bacon drippings until nicely brown on both sides. Serve with fried apples. It seems like apples, fried or applesauce, just naturally goes with pork.

When Marvin and I married during the Depression Days, he owned a small barber and beauty shop; both were very crude. He did have hydraulic barber chairs. Haircuts were 15¢, and shaves were 10¢. We set hair in cane-bottom chairs for 15¢, if you came with your hair already shampooed. It was 25¢, if we shampooed it. Permanents were $1.^{50}, except when on special they were $1.^{00}. Consequently, lots of bartering was done; labor for labor. Este McCall made this recipe for me; in this case, it was a permanent for mincemeat. I furnished the ingredients.

ORANGE MINCEMEAT
in memory of Este McCall

2 quarts apples
juice and rind of 4 oranges
    and 2 lemons
1 cup fruit juice
    (She probably used home
    canned peach pickle juice or
    juice from home canned peaches)
1 cup white beef suet (ground
    coarsely)
1 cup pecans
1 lb. raisins
1½ lbs. seedless raisins
    (She added some dried apicots)
1½ lbs. white sugar
1 tsp. each of allspice, nut
    meg, cinnamon
a little salt
2 slices of candied pineapples
    (cut into small bits)
¾ cup chopped citrus

Peel and core apples. They should be tart and juicy; chop, but not real fine. Peel the organges and lemons really thin and put them in the cup of fruit juice. Simmer the fruits and juices about 15 minutes and add the rest of the ingredients. Cook slowly for 30-40 minutes. Put in a tightly covered jar and keep in a cool dark place, or it can be put in sterilized jars and sealed. Now, you could refrigerate. It makes about 5 quarts.

My mother made fried pies for our school dinner bucket from the biscuits she made for the breakfast table. One biscuit made 1 pie and 1 rounded Tbsp. of mincemeat would be enough to fill 1 pie. To stretch 1 package of mincemeat, I add 1 can of crushed pineapple; it will make 2 pies. It is so good for cakes, cookies and anything else your imagination can come up with.

BUILDING A BRIDGE FOR HIM

An old man traveling a lone highway
Came at the evening cold and gray
To a chasm deep and wide

The old man crossed in the twilight dim,
For the sullen stream held no fears for him.
But he turned when he reached the other side,
And built a bridge to span the tide.

"Old man," cried a fellow pilgrim near,
"You are wasting your strength with building here;
Your journey will end with the ending day,
And you never again will pass this way."

"You have crossed the chasm deep and wide,
Why build you a bridge at eventide?"
And the builder raised his old gray head;
"Good friend, on the path I have come," he said,
"There followeth after me today,
A youth whose feet will pass this way."

"This stream which has been as naught to me,
To that fair-haired boy may a pitfall be;
He, too, must cross in the twilight dim
Good friend, I am building that bridge for him."

From "Rare Old Chums" by Ms. W. A. Dromgoole

POULTRY

GREAT PLANNING FOR SURVIVAL

Chicken was very important to our well being. It furnished food on the table. The eggs were fried in a skillet - left whole. My mother never turned them. She just flipped hot grease over them until the yolks were done. If we had company they were beaten together with some good cream and scrambled. Eggs wee traded to the Watkins salesman for spices and flavorings. We took them to the grocery to trade for soda, baking powder, sugar, or anything else.

The sponge cake and egg custard were so popular and were a good source of energy. Bread is said to be the staff of life was never truer than in those days and was served hot with every meal. There were boiled eggs for potato salad and deviled eggs for dinner on the ground and our school dinners. We raised our own wheat and corn. The corn was shelled and fed to the chickens and hogs. The corn had to be shelled after we got home from school. We could hardly wait until the roasting ears were ready to eat in the late Spring. The hot winds dried them up too early. We took our corn and wheat to the mill to have ground into meal and flour. When we had to buy it; it came in 48 lb. sacks.

The sacks had lots of uses. They were pieced into quilt linings and sometimes dyed. The sacks were often made into bed sheets. Curtains were made from sacks, enhanced with a gingham ruffle. In the Summer our panties were made from flour sacks, but they never had 48 lbs. printed on them. My mother took special pains to get the printing off. There was no Clorox in our house, so we just boiled them several times in that good lye soap. It wouldn't have made any difference if the printing had been left on. Our underwear was never seen. We were taught to put our dress down when we sat down. We could ride stick horses, but if we saw anybody coming we had to put them down. Modesty seems out of style these days.

Salt and sugar came in smaller sacks. They were used for dish rags and wash cloths. Most wash rags, as they were called, were made from old worn out towels. My mother would take the good part of cotton sacks and use for the men to dry their hands with when they were too dirty for our best towels. Marie and I even learned to embroidary on flour sacks that were hemmed and used for cup towels. Now back to the chickens.

We would raise two or three hundred chickens every year for the eggs and meat for the table. My father had regular customers in Mineral Well, Texas, (18 miles from home) for fresh eggs, buttermilk, fresh churned butter, and cream for whipping. Some would buy cream and do their own churning. My father would load up the buggy and do the chores early and be back home late. We would sell our products beginning in early Fall, because of no refrigeration. The eggs were packed in cotton seed to prevent breaking.

There were 7 children in my husband's family. Both of his parents came from large families. Their relatives were known to put their kids in the wagon; the neighbors would swap out doing the chores and come to see the Allens on Saturday and stay as late as they could on Sunday. Sometimes 3 or 4 cousins would stay. That's when you made big cobblers and "put the big pot in the little pot." My mother-in-law would raise a thousand chickens in the Spring. She often killed as many as a dozen chickens for Sunday dinner. They had lots of company.

The children didn't eat at the first tables. They didn't mind waiting. They were too busy playing, and besides she would put up choice pieces for the kids.

Chickens were stewed with a pot of those rolled flat dumplings, bake with cornbread dressing, made into scrapple, and smothered when they got too big to fry. And, of course, there was the ever popular "fried chicken" fried in that good lard. There is nothing any better than half lard and half butter to fry chicken in.

The article below is taken from a cookbook put out by the Southwest Utility Ice Company and was compiled by Maude Sims with the help of nutrition specialists from the A & M colleges of Oklahoma and Kansas. Aren't we glad we don't need these hints today? I, for one, know all about this method. I'm glad our daughters and granddaughters can follow much simpler instruction for frying chicken.

"It is wise to keep fowls up for a few days and feed on fattening rations, milk and grain if possible. This is done usually on the farm as the price paid for well fattened birds will justify the extra trouble of feeding awhile before selling. If produce houses buy birds that are not attended they usually feed and fatten them before selling to the butcher shops.

"Select a chicken that has a fine pliable skin or yellowish tint. If the bird is blue looking and hard to the touch, it is very likely to be an inferior specimen. Prepare by singeing and removing pin feathers, then wash it carefully. Unjoint in anyway desired and set in the icebox for a while before cooking. This will remove all remaining animal heat and greatly improve the finished product."

HINTS FOR FRYING THE BEST CHICKEN EVER

Dry carefully the chicken pieces. Dredge in flour with salt and pepper in a brown bag, a few pieces at a time. Use enough fat to half fill the skillet. I like half margarine and shortening. It should be hot enough to sizzle when the pieces are put in; but not too hot to shrink meat or toughen it.

If the grease is not hot enough, it will soak into the meat. When the chicken is browned evenly, lower the temperature to simmer. Cover and continue to cook chicken slowly. Turn often until chicken is tender and juicy. Always put the large pieces in the center. Pour off half of the fat toward the end of cooking. This can be used for gravy. Allow for gravy: 1 Tbsp. flour, 1 Tbsp. fat and 1 cup milk.

THE BEST FRIED CHICKEN EVER

chicken (disjoint)
2 cups flour
4 tsp. salt
½ tsp. black pepper

Pull chicken in flour mixture and fry according to the above directions. Make gravy and serve immediately. Good! Good! Good!

MRS. MILLS' ROAST TURKEY AND DRESSING

Before placing on a rack in an open roaster, cover the turkey with a paste. Cream together ¼ cup of soft butter (not melted), 5 Tbsp. of flour and 2 Tbsp. of lemon juice. This will look like whipped cream. Put heavy coating of this paste over the wings, breast and thigh joints. Also put a thin coating over the rest of the body. This will allow the turkey to brown nicely and be tender and moist.

DRESSING - This recipe makes a lot, so you can freeze some.

6 cups cornbread
4 cups stale whitebread (I use hamburger buns left out for a day to dry)
1½ cups celery (chopped)
1½ cups onions (chopped)
1 tsp. thyme
4 Tbsp. sage
4 eggs (beaten)
1 cup butter or oleo (melted)
pepper to taste

Steam onions and celery in butter in iron skillet. Do not brown. Crumble the bread mixture into bite sizes. Mix the bread crumbs with the seasoning and set overnight. Next morning, steam celery and onions, and add to bread mixture. Add a small amount of hot broth to moisten, then add melted butter and beaten eggs. Add more hot broth; just enough to make a dressing that will hold together. Press a handful of mixture into a ball that will hold together in your hand, but will break apart as it falls onto a plate. Then I know it has enough moisture to bake. Let it stand a few minutes. Add more broth if you think it needs it. Put in pan, well-greased, bake at 375° until done. Don't overcook.

GIBLET GRAVY

Pour off all fat from roast. Measure 4 Tbsp. of fat and return to roaster. Add 4 Tbsp. of flour which has been made into paste by adding a little cold water. Cook and brown well. Scrape all crustiness from sides of roaster. Cook flour well, but do not scorch. Use low heat. Add 2 cups of turkey broth. If you don't have 2 cups, finsih with water. Cook until smooth and thickened. Add chopped liver and gizzard. Some like chopped hard-cooked eggs. By this time you may want to take a short-cut and use a can of cream of chicken soup diluted with a little milk. It makes a good gravy. You can add the giblets now.

Cranberries originated in Massachusetts and are now grown in a few other seacoast states. They grow in bogs and are haravested without the help of commercial machinery. The tools are improvised by the growers. Cranberry sauce is traditional for Thanksgiving dinners.

CRANBERRY SAUCE

1 lb. cranberries
1 cup water
2 cups sugar
1 orange

Put the cranberries in a bowl of water. Pick out the faulty ones and any little sticks. Mix the water and sugar. Stir over medium heat until sugar is dissolved; boil for 5 minutes. Add the cranberries to sugar and cook just until the skins pop. Remove from heat, add juice and rind of 1 orange while hot. Stir well, cool, cover, and refrigerater.

MRS. MILLS' SPANISH BRAISED CHICKEN

Select a chicken of any vintage. Cooked by this method will be tender. Disjoint the fowl, dust with salt; be generous with pepper. Then dredge with flour. Then fry in skillet with butter until golden brown all over. Arrange in baking dish that has a tight fitting lid. In the same skillet make a sauce with:

4 Tbsp. butter
4 Tbsp. flour
2 cups broth
1 cup tomatoes
1 small clove garlic (minced)
salt and pepper to taste

Mix butter and flour together and cook slowly until slightly browned. Then add the stock and stir over a brisk fire until it is thickened. Add the next ingredients and pour over the chicken. Cover tightly. Bake in a slow oven at 300°-325° for 2 hours or until fork tender.

Ten minutes before serving saute' the following:

1½ cups mushrooms (diced)
1½ cup ripe olives
½ cup stuffed olives

Pour over the chicken and sprinkle with paprika.

FRIED CHICKEN IN MILK
circa 1935

¾ cup flour
4 tsp. salt
½ tsp. pepper
½ tsp. paprika
1 (2-3 lb.) frying chicken
　　(disjointed)
¼ - ½ cup butter
3-5 cups milk

Combine flour, salt, pepper and paprika in paper bag; shake chicken pieces until coated. Melt butter in a 12" frypan; fry chicken until golden brown on both sides. Remove frypan from heat. Pour milk over chicken to cover. Bake 350° for 1 hour.

OVEN BAG CHICKEN
OR TURKEY
Olevia Robinson

2 Tbsp. flour
1 medium onion (chopped)
16 lb. turkey

Preheat oven to 350°. Shake flour in oven bag and place in 2" roasting pan. Place vegetables in bag. Remove neck and giblets. Rinse bird and put in bag. Close bag with nylon tie. Bake for 2½ - 3½ hours for a 16" turkey.

CORNBREAD DRESSING
Olevia Robinson

3½ cup cornbread
3½ cup white bread
1½ cup butter (melted)
1 cup celery (chopped)
2 tsp. salt
½ tsp. pepper
½ tsp. savoring season
½ cup milk
2 cups chicken broth

Crumble bread in large bowl. Saute' onions and celery. Add to crumbs. Add other ingredients and mix well. If dressing seems too dry, add more broth. Bake in shallow pan at 350° for about 20-25 minutes.

PAN GRAVY
Olevia Robinson

Boil neck and giblets until tender. Remove bones and chop. Add salt and pepper and flour to thicken. About ¼ - ½ cup dissolved in milk. Add 1 can chicken broth. Add chopped boiled egg after gravy is thick.

MARIE MILLS' PAPRIKA CHICKEN

Disjoint about a 2½ lb. fryer. Boil giblets and neck in enough water to make 2 cups broth. You could add some chicken broth cubes. Dredge remaining pieces in flour and salt and pepper. Brown pieces on both sides in butter or fat if you prefer. Add a cup of chicken broth, a button of garlic and 2 Tbsp. of paprika. Don't let that shock you. It makes the dish. Cook the chicken and continue cooking for about 20 minutes. Add chicken broth as it evaporates. Turn chicken occasionally during first cooking. Remove the casserole cover, and cook until tender. Put in a serving dish. Then add 1 cup of thick cream (sweet or sour). Heat thoroughly. Stir until cream is mixed with paprika. Pour over chicken and serve.

CHICKEN SALAD
(congealed)

1 large chicken (cooked and boned)
6 hard cooked eggs
salt
cayenne pepper
3 Tbsp. vinegar
pepper

½ cup cold water
2 cups green pepper
1 can pimento
1 cup celery
1 pkg. gelatine
½-1 cup pecans

Cook and bone chicken. Save the broth. Chop fine. Mash eggs fine and mix with salt, cayenne, and vinegar. Soak 1 small pkg. of gelatine in cold water. Dissolve in hot broth. When mixture is cold and ready to set, add pecans, pimento, green pepper, and celery. Chop all real fine. Serve on lettuce leaf.

HOT CHICKEN SALAD
Olevia Robinson
another wonderful cook

2 cups cooked chicken breasts
1 cup celery (chopped)
1 can water chestnuts (sliced)
1 can cream of chicken soup
1 cup mayonaise
1 Tbsp. lemon juice

Mix and put into one 9"x12" baking dish. Put grated cheese and bread crumbs on top. Bake at 350°-400° for 20-30 minutes or until bubbly.

This recipe makes a good Sunday dinner. If you have a timer on your stove, set it to bake while at church.

CHICKEN BAKED IN RICE

1 frying chicken (disjointed)
salt and pepper to taste
1 cup rice
1 pkg. dry onion soap mix
2½ cup water
½ cup oleo

Season chicken with salt and pepper. Combine rice, soup mix and water. Arrange chicken over rice. Dot with oleo. Cover. Bake at 350° for about 1 hour and 15 minutes.

Try this, you can't believe how good it is. This is really great for company on a cold Winter Saturday evening. Mixed vegetables, your favorite green salad, and fruit salad would make a good menu. So good and satisfying and a real conservative dish.

STEWED CHICKEN WITH OLD TIMEY ROLLED DUMPLINGS

1 stewing hen
3 tsp. salt or less
pepper to taste
(You want plenty of broth.)

Place hen in deep kettle. Cover with water. Add 3 tsp. of salt and pepper to taste. Bring to a boil. Reduce heat, cover tightly. Simmer for at least 2 hours, or until hen is real tender. Hen could be cooked in pressure cooker if you are pressed for time. I prefer the simmer process. Remove chicken from broth; cool. Remove chicken from bones; chop. If the hen is real fat, refrigerate and take off surplus fat.

DUMPLINGS (rolled):

3 cups all-purpose flour
3 Tbsp. butter
2 Tbsp. shortening (slightly rounded)

Stir in just enough water or broth to make a stiff dough. Place on floured board. Knead until very stiff. Roll out dough, ¼ at a time, until paper thin. Cut into 2" strips. Bring broth to a boil. Add ¼ of the strips. Cook for about 5 minutes. Add remainng dough, ¼ at a time, bringing to a boil after each addition and stirring frequently. Cook untll dumplings are tender, adding boiling water to keep liquid soupy, if needed. Add chicken and butter. Cook until tender. Cover. It may take 10 or more minutes.

KITCHEN KAPERS: It takes longer to cook dumplings if you don't use baking powder, but they are much better.

MUSHROOM GRAVY

3 Tbsp. chicken fat or butter
3 Tbsp. flour
salt and pepper
2 cups chicken broth
1 cup milk
1 cup mushrooms (diced, fresh
    or cooked)

Blend the fat and flour with the seasonings. Add the broth and scalded milk and cook until smooth. Add the mushrooms that have been sauteed in butter. Serve over chicken, steak or whatever.

HARD BOILED EGGS

Recipes that call for hard boiled eggs should never be boiled. Put them in a saucepan (not aluminum) with enough cold water to cover eggs about 1". Let come to a fast rolling boil. Remove from heat and let stand, covered for 15 minutes. Cool quickly and peel. Eggs several days old will peel better.

This recipe was given to me by Jan Hall from Oklahoma City. It was given to her by her "nanna." She said it was a traditional Easter dish. It carried both her nanna and mother through The Depression Days. The eggs were cheap, available and plentiful, and very nutritious.

CREAMED EGGS

Boil and season the desired amount of potatoes. Prepare as you would mashed potatoes, milk, butter, salt and pepper. Whip until they form a peak when lifted up with a beater. Set aside.

Make a medium cream sauce. Boil and peel 8-10 eggs. Add chopped egg whites to the cream sauce. Make 3 layers in serving dish; first the whipped potatoes, then the cream sauce and then the mashed yolks. Continue until all is used, adding the yolks last. The number of potatoes you use depends on the amount of potatoes you prepare.

LADY BIRD JOHNSON'S BARBECUED CHICKEN

1- 1½-2 lb. broiler - fryer
salt and pepper to taste
¼ cup butter
¼ cup lemonjuice
¼ cup worcestershire sauce
¼ cup vinegar
¼ cup catsup

Cut chicken in quarters, wash and drain well. Sprinkle with salt and pepper. Place in a single layer in pan and broil under broiler until golden brown on both sides. Bring rest of ingredients to boil. Pour over chicken. Cook at 350° for 60 minutes. Baste often.

GOING TO THE GIN

One highlight of the Fall was going to the gin with our father sitting on top of that picked cotton in the wagon. If I remember right about 700 pounds made a bale. There is no one to confirm it. All the procedures were so fascinating. But the real treat was when our father went to the store and bought crackers; put up by the bulk, and cheese that we ate in the wagon. There was also some candy bars. We probably had water in a ½ gallon jug wrapped in a tow sack to keep cool. It was cold to begin with, fresh from the well. On the way home, my father stopped and let us pick some wild flowers for our mother. There were no vases; so they were put in syrup buckets or fruit jars.

BEEF

Beef is probably America's favorite meat, especially with men. It comes in a variety of cuts to suit every budget and taste. It's a rich souce of nutrients. Meat contains all 21 amino acids (building blocks) essential for growth and health maintenance, as well as, vitamins A, B6, B12, thiamine, riboflavin, and niacin. It tends to be high in calories, but the count can be reduced by carefully trimming off excessive fat before cooking.

All meat cookery is put into 2 catagories - moist heat and dry heat. Dry heat includes roasting and broiling. The more tender cuts of meat should be either roasted or broiled. To roast or broil always put in a roaster with fat side up. Roast uncovered in a moderate oven 325°-350°. No searing is necessary unless you want the brown crustiness that it adds to the roast. In that case you sear it first. You don't add any liquid. For a medium doness, cook 25 minutes per pound.

All the less tender cuts of meat are cooked by the long, slow moist method. This kind of meat requires a covering and no basting, because the lid holds the heat in. If you cook on top of the stove, cover and simmer. Use a moderate temperature 325° and allow 35 minutes cooking time per pound. For the liquid you can use heated meat juices, sour cream, any stock, and canned soup such as celery or mushroom. Use just enough hot liquid to keep plenty of steam for the meat, but not enough to swim in. Keep these 2 methods in mind, and you've got it made. I don't try to give you any hints on outdoor cooking; that's just not my "cup of tea."

MIKE ALLEN'S
CHICKEN FRIED STEAK

1 lb. round steak cut ¾" thick. Hack each piece with a heavy saucer. Soak about 30 minutes in buttermilk. Put 1½ cup flour and salt and pepper to taste in a paper bag. Put steak pieces in bag with flour mixture to

coat. Put in enough fat to nearly half fill the skillet. I like half butter and half lard. Let grease get hot enough to sizzle when meat is put in skillet. Let brown on both sides. Lower temperature and cook slowly for about 30 minutes. I always make gravy. There is none better than made from chicken fried steak. Please pass the biscuits.

MRS. MILLS' SWISS STEAK

1 large round steak 1" thick
2 cans mushrooms
½ tsp. garlic
1 tsp. salt
½ tsp. pepper
1 cup water
½ cup onions (chopped)
½ cup green pepper
        (chopped)
½ cup catsup
or
1 small can tomato sauce

Cut meat in seving pieces. Pound in flour, brown quickly on both sides. Place in heavy skillet. Add garlic, salt and pepper. Pour over enough water to prevent sticking while cooking. Cook and cover over low heat for 2 hours. Add mushrooms and liquid, onions, green pepper, catsup, or tomato sauce. Cook slowly for 1 hour. Last half hour leave lid off to let the juice boil down to thicken gravy.

HOT TAMALIE PIE
another meat stretcher

6 cups boiling water
2 cups cornmeal (I prefer yellow)
3 Tbsp. cooking fat
1 lb. ground meat
1 onion (chopped)
½ green pepper (chopped)
2 cups canned tomatoes
or
2 small cans of tomato sauce
salt and pepper to taste
add chili powder, if desired

Sift cornmeal slowly in rapid boiling water. Stir constantly. Cook 15 minutes. Brown ground meat, onion and gren pepper in hot fat. Add tomato sauce. Fill well oiled baking pan with alternate layers of cornmeal mush and meat mixture. Bake in hot oven (400°) for 20 minutes. Serve hot.

ONION SOUP MEATLOAF

2 lbs. ground chuck
1 envelope onion soup mix
2 eggs (beaten)
½ cup catsup
1½ cup soft bread crumbs
¾ cup warm water

Mix all ingredients with soup mix with a hand mixer. Bake in loaf pan at 350° for 1 hour. Make bread crumbs in mixer. 1½ cup oatmeal may be used or about 1½ cups cracker crumbs instead of the soft bread crumbs.

MEATBALLS WITH TOMATO GRAVY

1 lb. hamburger
¼ lb. pork sausage
2 Tbsp. onion (chopped)
1 cup soft bread cubes
cayenne pepper
paprika
1 clove garlic (chopped)
2 eggs (well-beaten)
4 cups tomato juice
¼ tsp. nutmeg

Combine hamburger, sausage, nutmeg, bread cubes, onion, garlic, eggs, and a few grains of cayenne pepper and paprika. Mix thoroughly. Season to taste. Form in small balls. Roll in flour. Heat tomato juice to boiling. Season with salt and pepper. Drop meatballs into boiling tomato juice. Cover and simmer for 40 minutes. Serves 8.

This is a good way to use left over meat. Serve with a salad and dessert. You will have a good meal. I've had lots of calls for this recipe.

SHEPHERD PIE
in memory of Estie McCall

4 Tbsp. cooking fat
3 Tbsp. onion (chopped)
2 Tbsp. green peppers
½ cup celery (diced)
1 cup cooked meat (diced)
4 Tbsp. flour
2 cups milk or meat stock
½ cup cooked carrots
(diced)

Slowly brown onion, pepper, celery, and meat in cooking faat, stirring constantly. Add flour slowly, stir until brown. Add remaining ingredients. Heat thoroughly. Put in a shallow well-greased baking dish. Cover with a layer of well-seasoned mashed potatoes. Dot with butter.

MEAT SALAD
good for left-overs

2 cups cooked meat (diced)
1 cup cooked potatoes
(cubed), carrots, peas or
beets
½ cup mayonaise
2 eggs (hard cooked)
1 onion (minced)
½ cup sweet pickles
(chopped)
salt and pepper

Combine all ingredients. Season to taste. Mix lightly with fork. Serve on lettuce leaf with hot rolls and butter.

Another good way to use left over meat.

MEAT PIE

4 Tbsp. cooking oil
3 Tbsp. onion (chopped)
2 Tbsp. green peppers
	(chopped)
½ cup celery (diced)
1 cup cooked meat (diced)
4 Tbsp. flour
2 cups milk or beef stock
1½ cup cook carrots (diced)

Slowly brown onion, pepper, celery, add meat, in cooking fat, stiring constantly. Add flour, stirring constantly, until brown. add remaining ingredients. Heat thoroughly. Pour into a shallow well-oiled baking pan. Cover with biscuits. Bake in hot oven (400°) about 15 minutes or until biscuits are done.

Diane Messinger from Bellevue, Michigan, shared this recipe with me. She says it's "the best."

BEEF BRISKET

1 (5-6 lb.) beef brisket
3 Tbsp. cooking oil
2 cups onion (chopped)
4 stalks celery (chopped, including leaves)
2 round tsp. crumbled beef bouillon
1 green pepper cut in strips
2 cloves garlic
or
½ tsp. garlic powder
1 tsp. paprika
½ tsp. fresh milled pepper
2 Tbsp. fresh dill leaves
or
1 tsp. dried dill leaves
2 bay leaves (cut in half)
2 cups favorite red wine and/or grape juice or water
2 Tbsp. vinegar
2 lbs. of small whole potatoes (or canned)
2 lbs. fresh medium parsnips
4 carrots cut lengthwise and in half
½ bunch parsley
2 medium ripe tomatoes

Remove extra fat. Brown well in roasting pan or dutch oven. Cook up onions, celery and green peppers, so they are well wilted; low flame so the flavors intermingle. Put side of the meat up, sprinkle with paprika, garlic, beef bouillon, dill, pepper, and place bay leaves around meat. Then take half the fried mixture and place on the bottom of the roaster and put the meat on top; then put the other half of the fried mixture on top of the meat. Add wine or other liquid and vinegar. Cover and put in a 325° oven for 3-3½ hours. Add more liquid if necessary, add carrots, parsnips and potatoes around meat and cook 30 minutes more. Taste and adjust salt. Wait 15 minutes, slice across the grain. Garnish with parsley and tomatoes. Serve with vegetables and juice.

"Wise men lay up knowledge: but the mouth of the foolish is near destruction."
Proverbs 10:14

BARBECUED SHORT RIBS
(beef)

1½-2 lbs. short ribs
2 stalks celery (chopped)
1 med. onion (minced)
1 Tbsp. sugar
½ cup catsup
1 Tbsp. vinegar
¼ tsp. sauce
¼ tsp. chili powder
pepper to taste
½ tsp. salt
1 cup water

Place ribs in roaster. Combine celery, onion, sugar, catsup, vinegar, hot sauce, and water. Pour over ribs. Add more water, if sauce does not cover ribs. Cover. Bake at 350° for 2-3 hours or until tender. Yields 4-6 servings.

SKILLET SUPPER

2 large onions (thinly sliced)
2 strips of bacon
        (cut in ½ pieces)
1 lb. ground beef
2 med. potatoes (cut in strips)
1 green pepper (cut in strips)
2 cups cabbage (shreaded)

2 stalks celery (diced)
2 medium tomatoes
¼ cup soy sauce
½ cup water

Fry bacon pieces until crisp. Add onions and beef and cook until browned. Add vegetables in layers and cover with soy sauce and water. Cover and boil 1 minute. Reduce heat and simmer about 15 minutes or until vegetables are done. Yields 4 servings.

BEST ROAST

5-7 lb. rump roast. Rub the roast with suet and heat until very hot. Sear meat on all sides. Add about ¼-½ cup water. Cover with tight lid. Cook at 300° for 35 minutes per pound. There will be plenty broth for rice or noodles. Good for sandwiches. You can add potatoes or carrots or whole onions around roast. Try searing roast with kidney suet. Makes a world of difference in taste. You've got it made! Good for getting or keeping your man.

MRS. MILLS' BURRY RUMP ROAST

5-7 lbs. beef rump roast
¾-1 lb. ham from hock or end
pieces

Marinade:

3 parts of oil to 1 part of vinegar
1 clove of garlic (split)
½ cup each of stock
tomato catsup
a few celery leaves
a slice or 2 of carrots

Trim the fat from beef. Cut ham in ¼"
pieces then into 1¾" strips long. Gash
the meat and insert the ham strips.
Bits of the ends will protrude, giving
the meat a burry appearance.
Marinate the roast in the oil and vinegar for an hour or longer, turning several times. Insert the garlic. rub the
roast with suet and heat until very
hot. Sear on all sides. Add the hot
stock and catsup mixed with the celery leaves and carrot. Cover with a
tight lid. Cook at 325° allowing 35
minutes to the pound. No matter
how you cook rump roast, you can't
go wrong. If there is any left, you can
use barbecue sauce, make hash, or
it slices perfectly for sandwiches. Try it
on rye bread.

This recipe is really good for Saturday night get-togethers. Serve with a green toss salad, a slice of garlic bread and for dessert - small slice of pound cake.

BROILED HAMBURGER STEAK ON ONION RINGS

7 large slices of Spanish onion
        (cut ½" thick)
3 Tbsp. butter (melted)
1 Tbsp. parsley (chopped)
1 cup soft bread crumbs
1 Tbsp. water
1 tsp. salt
black and cayenne pepper
        to taste
1 lb. lean beef (finely
chopped)
7 slices of bacon

Butter a shallow baking dish. Lay the slices of onions in dish and add the melted butter. Sprinkle with salt and pepper. Cover the dish tightly and bake in 350° oven for 30 minutes or until onions are done. Add the pars-ley, crumbs, water, and seasonings to the chopped meat. Shape into 7 flat cakes. Wrap each cake with a slice of bacon. Place each patty on slice onion. Run it under broiler for about 5 minutes. Turn meat patty and broil on the other side. Serve piping hot.

If you have never cooked cabbage like this, you are in for a surprise!

LOIS ALLEN'S CABBAGE WITH CORN BEEF

1 head cabbage (about 2 lbs.)
1½ cups boiling water
1¼ tsp. salt
¼ cup butter (melted)
1 can corned beef (12 oz.)
1 can whole kernel corn
salt to taste
a dash of cayenne pepper

Cut the cabbage through the center into 6 sections, leaving the head intact at the core end. Tie loosely with a string and place in the salted boiling water. Cover and steam until cabbage is tender - about 20 minutes. Do not overcook. Use a sharp knife and remove the core which portrudes in the center. Put on a platter and remove the string. Pour over the cabbage the ¼ cup of melted butter. In the meantime heat the corned beef and corn together. Pour corned beef and corn mixture in center of cabbage on platter. Season the cabbage and corn mixture with cayenne pepper. Serve with a rich white sauce (page 77). You might add a bit of horseradish. Listen for the "ohs and ahs."

This makes a good evening meal with crackers or cornbread and a simple dessert.

MRS. WHITE'S BEEF STEW
circa 1940

1½ lbs. beef chuck (cubed)
1 tsp. shortening
1 clove of garlic (minced)
½ tsp. salt
⅛ tsp. pepper
1 can of tomatoes (crushed)
3 med. carrots
3 med. potatoes
1 med. onion
3 stalks celery
a dash of hot sauce or
        cayenne pepper
¼ tsp. powdered basil
¼ tsp. powdered thyme

Slightly brown the beef in shortening. Peel and chop all vegetables. Place in large stew pan with plenty boiling water to which the meat has been added. Cook under medium heat for about 25 minutes. Add herbs and simmer 30 minutes longer. Salt to taste. Sometimes I add ½ cup long grain rice about 30 minutes before done. I also add about 2 tsp. of bouillon cubes. This will make a lot and keeps really good. You can freeze some.

CREOLE GUMBO

2½ cups diced okra
1 lb. brisket (diced)
1 bay leaf
3 sprigs of parsley (chopped)
        can use dehydrated
½ cup of cooking fat
½ onion (chopped)
½ lb. ham (chopped)
2 cups canned tomatoes
6 cups boiling water
2 Tbsp. flour salt, pepper and
        cayenne pepper to taste
1 green pepper

Brown ham and brisket in cooking fat. Remove meat. Brown okra and onion in fat. Add flour slowly; still until blended. Add meat and remaining ingredients, stirring constantly. Season to taste. Cover. Simmer slowly until meat is tender. Serve hot over steamed rice. Serves 6.

This recipe isn't used in my part of the country. As a matter of fact, I've never heard of it, until I began showing my cookbook in th South. I've had lots of call for it. So here it is.

LIVER DUMPLINGS

1½ lbs. beef liver
1 Tbsp. butter
1 large onion (diced)
8 cups bread crumbs

2 eggs (beaten)
salt and pepper to taste
½ cup flour
6 cups beef or chicken broth

Cook liver in small amount of water for 5 minutes. Remove from pan and grind. Melt butter in large skillet. Saute' onions and crumbs n butter. Combine liver and eggs; add to crumb mixture. Season with salt and pepper. Stir in flour. Pour broth in large saucepan; bring to a boiling point. Drop liver mixture by spoonfuls into hot broth. Cook covered for 30 minutes. shaking frequently. Soup may be substituted for broth.

LOIS ALLEN'S BAR-B-QUE SAUCE
FOR BRISKET
the best ever

6 Tbsp. brown sugar
2 Tbsp. dry mustard
a dash of nutmeg
1 cup catsup
2 tsp. lemon juice
2 Tbsp. soy sauce

Either add to meat before cooking or serve with meat. If served over meat, heat slightly.

FOODS THAT MEN LIKE

BARBECUE MEATBALLS

¼ cup onion (finely chopped)
1 garlic cloves (crushed)
1 Tbsp. butter or margarine
3 Tbsp. vinegar
¼ cup sugar
4 tsp. worcestershire sauce
1 tsp. salt
½ tsp. pepper
1 tsp. paprika
1 (14 oz.) bottle of catsup
½ cup water

SAUCE:

Saute' onion and garlic in butter in medium saucepan until onion is tender. Add remaining ingredients; combine thoroughly. Cook over real low heat while preparing meatballs.

MEATBALLS:

1½ lb. ground beef
¾ cup uncooked quick oats
1½ tsp. salt
¼ tsp. pepper
2 Tbsp. onion (finely chopped)
1 egg
1 cup milk

For meat balls. Combine all ingredients thoroughly. Shape to form 12 meatballs about 2 inches across. Brown well on all sides in small amount of shortening. Drain off excess fat. Pour sauce over meatballs. Reduce heat, cover and simmer for about 30 minutes. Occasionally spoon sauce over meatballs. Serves 6.

This is my favorite way to make chili - without onions and tomatoes.

BLUE RIBBON STATE FAIR CHILI

1 Tbsp. shortening
2 lb. ground beef
4 tsp. finely chopped garlic
1 small bottle chili powder
2 Tbsp. flour
1 tsp. ground camino seed
1 Tbsp. salt
¼ tsp. pepper

Heat shortening in frying pan until hot. Add ground beef and finely choped garlic. Cover. Reduce heat to low. Let beef mixture simmer for about 15 minutes. Mix chili powder, flour and camino seed together. Add to beef mixture. Stir well. Add 3 cups water; season with salt and pepper. Simmer for 35 minutes. Serves 8-10.

SERMONS WE SEE

"I'd rather see a sermon
than hear one any day,

I'd rather one should walk with me
than merely show the way.

The eye's a better pupil
and more willing than the ear;

Fine counsel is confusing,
but example's always clear;

And the best of all the preachers
are the men who live their creeds.

For to see the good in action
is what everybody needs.

I can soon learn how to do it
if you'll let me see it done.

I can watch your hands in action,
but your tongue too fast may run.

And the lectures you deliver
may be very wise and true;

But I'd rather get my lesson
by observing what you do.

For I may misunderstand you
and the high advice you give,

But there's no misunderstanding
how you act and how you live."

by Edgar A. Guest

FISH

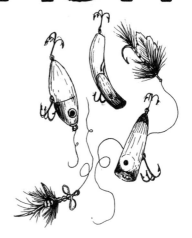

BATTERED CATFISH

I lb. medium catfish fillets
melt
1 cup shortening
1 cup oleo
in a medium frying pan
mix
½ cup milk
1 egg
cornmeal
season fish with salt and pepper

Dip fillets into milk mixture, then roll in meal. Drop in hot shortening and fry until brown (about 7 minutes). Turn once. Serve with Hush Puppies and Cabbage Slaw.

Hush Puppies have been said to have derived their name from a Southern activity. At fish fries, Southerners would quite their hungry dogs' whining by throwing them scraps of fried cornmeal batter and say "hush puppy" to their dogs.

BUTTERMILK HUSH PUPPIES

1½ cup cornmeal
½ cup flour
4 green onions (chopped)
1 egg
⅛ tsp. salt
2 tsp. baking powder
½ tsp. soda
1 cup buttermilk
4 Tbsp. bacon drippings

Mix add ingredients and drop by spoonfuls into deep hot fat in heavy skillet. Fry until golden brown.

SOUR CREAM HALIBUT

1½ lbs. halibut
1 stick butter or margarine
paprika
salt and pepper to taste
2 cups sour cream
1 lb. cheddar cheese (shreaded)
1 package almonds (slivered)

Rinse fish and pat dry. Dip in butter and sprinkle both sides with paprika, salt and pepper. Place in baking dish. Bake at 350° for about 30 minutes or until fish flakes easily. Drain off butter, but leave a little in bottom of pan. Completely cover fish with sour cream. Spread grated cheese over until dish. Sprinkle almonds on top. Return to oven until cheese melts (about 10-12 minutes). Cabbage slaw is always good with fish. Serve with French bread.

QUICK SALMON CROQUETTES

1 can salmon
crushed cornflakes
2 eggs (beaten)
1 tsp. baking powder
1 tsp. salt

Drain salmon, reserve liquid. Flake salmon; remove skin and bones. Combine salmon, reserved liquid, egg, salt, and enough cornflakes to make a firm mixture. Add baking powder. Shape into croquettes; roll into additional cornflakes. Fry in small amount of fat in skillet until lightly browned.

SALMON LOAF

1- 1 lb. can salmon
1 can celery soup
2 eggs (beaten)
2½ cups soft brad crumbs or
        crackers
1 hard cooked egg (chopped)
3 tsp. pickle relish
1 cup thin white sauce (heated)
¼ tsp. onion powder

Drain and flake salmon; remove skin and bones. Add soup, eggs and crumbs. Mix lightly. Turn into a greased 8½"x4½" greased loaf pan. Bake for 1 hour. Mix remaining ingredients. Serve sauce over loaf. Serves 6.

SALMON NOODLE CASSEROLE

2 cups salmon
1½ cups medium white sauce
1 cup cooked noodles
salt and pepper
¼ cup buttered bread crumbs
       or crackers

Drain salmon. Flake. Remove all bones and skin. Fill well-oiled baking dish with alternate layers of salmon, white sauce and noodles. Season each layer. Cover with bread or crackers crumbs. Bake in moderate oven (375°) for about 30 minutes. Serves 6.

TARTAR SAUCE

1 cup mayonnaise dressing
1 Tbsp. dill pickles (chopped)
1 Tbsp. olives (chopped) optional
1 tsp. parsley (chopped)
1 Tbsp. grated onion (just enough
       for flavor)

Serve at once. Serve with broiled, baked, steamed, or fried fish.

BARBECUED STUFFED SHRIMP

2 Tbsp. butter
2 Tbsp. onion (chopped)
2 Tbsp. celery (chopped)
2 Tbsp. green pepper
        (chopped)
2 Tbsp. flour
½ cup milk
¼ cup bread crumbs
1 cup cooked crabmeat
1½ tsp. Worcestershire sauce
1½ tsp. parsley (chopped)
¼ tsp. salt
¼ tsp. pepper
3 doz. large shrimp

Melt butter in skillet. Saute' first 4 ingredients with medium heat. Mix flour and milk, stirring constantly until thick. Add bread crumbs and crabmeat, Worcestershire sauce, chopped parsley, salt, and pepper. Mix well. Remove shell and vein from shrimp. Put 2 shrimp together with crab stuffing. Hold together with toothpicks. Chill until ready to cook. Place shrimp into broiler pan 5 inches from broiler unit. Baste with barbecue sauce until shrimp are done; about 5 minutes on each side.

BARBECUE SAUCE

1 Tbsp. fat
2 Tbsp. onion (chopped)
2 Tbsp. vinegar
2 Tbsp. brown sugar
1 cup catsup
⅓ cup lemon juice
½ tsp. salt
a dash of hot sauce
3 Tbsp. Worcestershire sauce

Saute' onion in fat. Add other ingredients and simmer for 5 minutes on low heat. Yields 6 servings.

THE GOLDEN YEARS

Oh, I know I'm growing older,
  And the years just fly away,
But my hours are filled with sunshine,
  For I live for God each day.

I don't have time to spend complaining
  Of what fate has done to me.
I must be about my father's business;
  He still has work for me, you see.

I might lift another' s spirits
  With a phone call or a smile;
Maybe some poor soul in sorrow
  Needs a friend for just a while.

Perhaps some youth besieged by trouble
  Needs the wisdom of my years;
It's a treasure that was purchased
  With a million silver tears.

Yes, I know I'm growing older;
  Threescore years I've lived and ten,
And my journey's almost finished
  Through this wilderness of sin.

But I know my loving master;
  Through the years he's stilled my fears,
Lent his balm to all my heartaches,
  Wiped away the stinging tears.

And if tonight dark death should call me,
  All my earthly ties should sever,
Home I'd fly to heaven's mansion,
  There with God to live forever!

From "Echoes From My Heart" by Ed Lobaugh

Ed Lobaugh is the minister of the Elm and Hudson Street Church of Christ, Altus, Oklahoma, where I have attended for over 60 years.

FRUITS

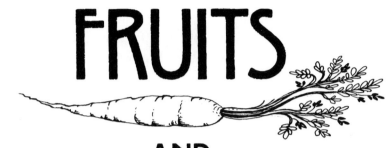

AND

VEGETABLES

BEANS

I'm sure there were tons of pinto beans served during *The Great Depression* without knowing how nutritious they were. It was always served with cornbread and plently of freshly churned butter. If we didn't have fried chicken (home-grown), we had fried potatoes fried in lard we rendered from the hog killing days. Then there was chow chow; made especially to eat with pinto beans. If there was time, there might be a cobbler made from home canned fruit, such as wild plums, wild green grapes or peaches.

The wash tub was put under the roof to catch rainwater to cook the beans in, since they were so much softer cooked in rainwater that had to be strained. They were soaked overnight, and the water was poured off when ready to cook. They were cooked with high heat until they reached a rolling boil. Then the heat was reduced to just below simmering. About 30 minutes before they are tender, add ham or sausage that has been fried in sliced salt pork. Then you added all the grease and seasoning from the skillet, cover and cook until the beans were tender. Before the beans were done, you uncover them and cook on a medium fire to give them a creamy texture. Stir often to keep the beans from sticking. If you wanted the soup to be thicker, take out ¼ cups of beans, mash with a spoon and add to the beans. If the salt seasonings were added too soon, it would toughen the beans. Always add boiling water to the beans. Cold water will also toughen the beans. If you will follow these directions, you'll have beans fit for a king. They must be served with fresh green onions. If not available, use sliced raw onion rings.

MARVIN ALLEN'S
PINTO BEANS AND RICE

1 lb. dried pinto beans
1 large onion (chopped)
4 stalks celery (chopped)
4 cloves garlic (chopped)
2 bay leaves
2 Tbsp. Worcestershire sauce
Tabasco sauce to taste
1 large slice of center cut ham
        (cut in small pieces or
        salt pork)
4-6 cups cooked rice (long
        grain, cook according
        to package directions)

Pick and wash beans in a colander. Put in a 3 quart pan and cover the beans about 3 inches above the beans with boiling water. Cover and let beans set for at least an hour. Drain what water is left. Fill with hot water until the beans are covered by several inches. Put on high heat and bring quickly to a rolling boil. Do not cover. Put another pot of water on the stove and cover it with a lid (so that the water won't boil away quickly), bring to a boil, then reduce to simmer. This is water to replenish the big bean pot as it boils down. Boil the beans for about 2 hours. Add the chopped celery, onion, bay leaves, and garlic. Continue to cook

just above a simmer. Watch carefully. Do not let the beans get too dry or
they will stick. As the water is
reduced in the pot, bring the second
pot of simmering water to a full boil
and add to the beans. If you add
cold water, instead of boiling water
to the beans, they will be tougher.
Continue cooking the beans until the
water is half gone. Stir occasionally
to keep the beans from sticking. Now
is the time to cover and add these
ingredients: celery, ham, and
Worcestershire sauce. Tabasco
sauce could be added if desired. If
the salt seasoning is added before
the beans are nearly done, the salt
will make them tough. Cook until tender. Serve over white rice.

POTATO ANNA
(from an old cookbook by the Wilson
Meat Packing Company)

Wash and pare 6 medium potatoes,
trimming into cylinder shapes. Cut
into slices about ⅛" thick in diameter.
Freshen in cold water and dry on a
towel. Butter the bottom of a skillet
and arrange the potatoes to have
the slips overlap each other. The
bottom layer becomes the top
when the potatoes are turned out,
so arrange them nicely. Cover the

entire bottom of the pan. Spread each layer with softened butter and season each layer with salt and pepper. Continue to build each layer until about 2" high. Cover pan and bake in 350° oven for about 1 hour. Remove from oven. Uncover pan and place large plate on top; invert pan carefully, and you will have a rounded batch of potatoes with a golden browned top.

AUNT ANNA'S SCALLOPED POTATOES

2 Tbsp. butter
2 Tbsp. flour
1 tsp. salt
⅛ tsp. pepper
2 cups milk
4 medium sliced potatoes
1 medium size onion

Make a white sauce by using the top 5 ingredients. In a small saucepan, melt the butter. Blend in the flour, salt and pepper. Gradually add the milk. Cook until it thickens (above 10 minutes). Scrub the potatoes, peel and slice thin. Peel onion and slice thin. Place alternating layers of potatoes, sauce and onions in a greased 1½ quart casserole. Bake in moderate oven for 1-1½ hours, or until the potatoes are tender. Bake covered, add more milk if needed to brown. Remove lid the last few minutes.

This isn't really a salad, but a hot potato dish that the Germans brought to us. It is good with ham or fried pork chops. Serve with fresh or frozen spinach. This will "stick to your ribs" as we say in the South. It also gives you quick energy.

GERMAN HOT POTATO SALAD

6-8 good sized potatoes
3 Tbsp. bacon drippings
1 large onion (chopped)
½ cup celery (chopped)
½ pint heavy cream
½ cup cider vinegar
½ tsp. dry mustard
2 tsp. salt
½ tsp. pepper

Wash potatoes well; boil them with their jackets on for about 40 minutes or until tender. While potatoes are boiling, saute' the onion and celery in the bacon fat until tender. Heat the vinegar with the cream, mustard, salt, and pepper. Do not boil. Drain the potatoes. Peel them while they are hot and slice them in a wooden salad bowl. Mix well with the onion and vinegar dressing. Serve hot with buttered spinach.

This Kitchen Kaper was always done when we lived on the farm and raised potatoes in the garden.

KITCHEN KAPERS: To keep old potatoes, not intended for seed, from sprouting and withering, place in a gunnysack and lower in boiling water for 2 or 3 minutes. Move them about so the water will reach all parts of the surface. Lay them out on a flat surface to dry thoroughly before storing. The boiling water kills the germs. Potatoes treated this way will keep until a new crop comes in.

70

BUTTERED SPINACH

2-3 boxes frozen spinach (cook
    according to directions)
toss with
4 Tbsp. butter
salt and pepper to taste
⅛ tsp. nutmeg

Garnish with hard boiled egg slices.
Place a cruet of good vinegar or
peppersauce on table. Don't forget
the hot buttered cornbread.

There are so many different ways to serve potatoes, but we are prone to resort to just a few ways. Why not try the potato croquette occasionally. It's a good way to use left over mashed potatoes.

MARIE MILLS'
POTATO CROQUETTES

2 cups hot potatoes (mashed)
2 Tbsp. butter
2 egg yolks
½ tsp. salt
¼ tsp. pepper
small amount of grated onion

Mix and beat all ingredients together.
Shape into croquettes and dip into fine
bread crumbs, then into slightly beaten
egg and again in bread crumbs. Fry in
deep hot fat until nicely browned. Fat
should be hot enough to brown an inch
cube of bread in 1 minute. Drain on
unglazed paper and sprinkle with salt.

This recipe was popular in the '20s and the Depression era. It was jokingly said if our blood was tested back then, it would be 50% black-eye pea juice.

BLACK-EYED PEAS PATTIES
in memory of Este McCall

Mix
2 tsp. onions (finely grated)
2 tsp. lemon juice
3 dashes of cayenne pepper
2 tsp. butter (melted)
2 cups sieved cooked black-
    eyed peas
2 eggs
flour

Mix well and this can be used as a spread on hot crackers or on thin cornmeal fried cakes. Or you can add 2 beaten frothy eggs; save whites of one. Mix in 2 Tbsp. of flour. Make into patties. Roll in egg white and then into cracker crumbs or bread crumbs. Fry in about ¼" of hot grease.

SAUSAGE BAKED APPLES

Peel a tart apple and hollow them out with an apple corer. Leave an opening about ½" thick. Sprinkle all over with lemon juice to keep them from discoloring. Fill in the centers with sausage. Do not pack. Bake in a covered dish in 350° oven for an hour. Remove the lid, brush with butter, sprinkle lightly with sugar on top and continue baking

This recipe can be used as a main dish if used with any good brand of sausage in a casing - sliced or fried with it or a side dish without sausage.

FRIED CABBAGE
Helen Long

Cut cabbage in half and then into wedges. Fry in bacon drippings; turning as it fries. When wilted, add ¼ - ⅓ cup of water. Add salt, pepper and sugar, if desired. Steam for a few minutes with a lid. Don't peep. It's really good.

MARIE MILLS' SPICED CARROTS

Steam desired amount of carrots until tender. Leave 2 Tbsp. of liquid in carrots. Combine 2 Tbsp. sugar with ¼ cup vinegar and 4-5 whole cloves to steamed carrots. Pour sauce over carrots and steam for about 2 minutes. Remove from heat, cover and let set 5 minutes before serving.

APRICOT SAUCE
in memory of Zora Baker

¼ lb. dried apricots
1 can (large) pineapple

Wash apricots and cover with 1½ cups cold water and soak for 1-2 hours. Simmer until tender. Add pineapple and heat until sauce is desired sauce consistency. Mash apricots before adding pineapple. Good with biscuits.

This is a beautiful edible garnish for ham, sausage or bacon.

POACHED APPLE RINGS
Pansy Spear

1 cup water
1½ cups sugar
½ cup white corn syrup
3 Tbsp. lemon juice
2 lbs. tart, just ripe red apples

Put first 4 ingredients into a 10" aluminum skillet or a shallow saucepan. Stir thoroughly. Simmer for 5 minutes. Wash and remove stem and blossom ends, core and then cut apples into ⅜" slices crosswise. Slide apples into boiling syrup. Continue simmering until apples are tender and translucent. Lift out with spatula. You may use syrup again by adding a little more syrup, sugar and water.

MRS. MILLS'
OLD TIME CRANBERRIES

2 cups sugar
2 cups water
1 quart cranberries
a dash of salt

Pick over cranberries, discard damage ones. Wash in cold water and drain. Measure sugar and water into a 3 quart saucepan. Heat to boiling point. Reduce heat and boil slowly for 5 minutes. Now add berries, salt, cover and simmer for 5 minutes without stirring. Remove from heat. Cool in pan; keep covered.

BROCCOLI RICE CASSEROLE
in memory of Gladys Brown

½ cup onions (chopped)
½ cup celery (chopped)
1 cup rice (long grain, raw)
1 package chopped broccoli
1 can cream of mushroom soup
1 can cream of celery soup
1 small jar Cheese Whiz
paprika

Saute' onions and celery. Cook rice and broccoli separately. If long grain rice is used, use ¾ cup and cook according to directions. Mix the vegetables, add soups and Cheese Whiz. Place rice in casserole as a lining for dish. Pour vegetable mixture over it and sprinkle with paprika. Bake at 375° for 10-15 minutes before serving. May be prepared a day or two ahead of time. Good with fried chicken and gravy and a tossed salad.

SCALLOPED ASPARAGUS
Ruth McLauglin

2 cups cooked asparagus
1 cup grated cheese
salt and pepper
4 hard cooked eggs
1½ cups medium white sauce
paprika

Fill well-oiled baking dish with alternate layers of asparagus, cheese, white sauce, and sliced eggs. Sprinkle with salt and pepper and paprika. Bake in moderate oven for about 20 minutes. Serves 6.

ZUCCHINI SOUR CREAM CASSEROLE

Cut 3 small zucchinis in fairly small pieces lengthwise and then quarter. Simmer and cover with small amount of water until barely tender for about 6 - 8 minutes. Then combine 1 Tbsp. butter, ½ cup grated cheese, ½ tsp. salt. I use less; the cheese will be salty. Add ¼ tsp. paprika. Stir over low heat until cheese is melted. Take from heat and stir quickly 1 beaten egg and 1 Tbsp. chives.

It would make "everyday cooking" a lot easier, if you would memorize these basic recipes for sauces.

THIN WHITE SAUCE

1 cup milk (scalded)
1 Tbsp. butter (melted)
1 Tbsp. flour
½ tsp. salt
pepper

Combine butter and flour. Add milk slowly, stirring constantly. Cook over hot water or heavy saucepan until thick and smooth. Add salt and pepper. Use in soups.

MEDIUM WHITE SAUCE

1 cup milk (scalded)
2 Tbsp. flour
2 Tbsp. butter (melted)
½ tsp. salt
pepper

Follow directions for this sauce. Use for creamed and scalloped dishes.

THICK WHITE SAUCE

1 cup milk (scalded)
3 Tbsp. flour
3 Tbsp. butter (melted)
½ tsp. salt
pepper

Follow directions for thin white sauce. Use for souffles.

GARDENING

Everybody in the olden days raised a garden, even if you lived in town. There was nothing to compare to the taste of those vine-riped tomatoes. I can still taste those fresh English peas with the creamsauce made from fresh cream and those newly dug potatoes. We didn't peel the new potatoes, just scraped them with a knife. A "Chore Girl" would have been great, but we didn't didn't have one.

Seeds were saved from one year to the next. If we had to buy seed, they were ordered from a catalog. There were a few colored pages - so pretty! The tomato seed was planted in a wood box and kept in the house. When they came up, the plants were put put in the window where they could get sunshine. At the proper time, they were transplanted to the garden. The ripe tomatoes were canned and used in soups and macaroni. In the Fall before the green tomatoes froze, we fried them and made them into pies and cakes, green tomato mincemeat, and chow chow to eat with those dried beans and black-eyed peas. Those beans and peas were mighty good, too.

Okra grew really well. We fried it and put it stews. Okra was cooked with onions, tomatoes and boiled salt pork. I still fry potatoes, squash, okra, and onion (added last) in the small skillet. When we were on the farm in the Spring, the family could always have fried chicken with that good cream gravy. There was always a big skillet of cornbread. Nothing compares to that food. We never heard of cholesterol. It really didn't matter, because we worked it off.

DESSERTS

MAKING MOLASSES

There had to be a lot of planning for the farmer to produce good tasting molasses. Selecting a good cane seed and finding a good location for the cane patch were most important. The cane patch needed to have sandy soil and be well drained. After planting and cultivating, you had to remove the blades from each stalk by hand in order for the molasses to have a bright color and better taste. Each stalk was cut and laid in piles to dry for a few days. The heads (seed) were cut with a knife and stored for chicken feed. The cane stalks were loaded on the wagon and taken to the cane mill. The harvesting had to be done before the first frost arrived. If you became thristy while harvesting, you could twist or peel open the stalk and suck out the great tasting juice.

The cane mill had large rollers for squeezing the juice from the stalks. The rollers were turned by a horse or mule that was hitched to a long wooden sweep which allowed the animal to walk in a circle. Cane juice would fill a large reservoir. The juice was strained, and then it flowed to the cooking pan. It ran slightly downhill, back and forth in the pan. The large pan with several compartments was set over a large furnace and heated by long slabs of wood. Cane left over after being fed through the press was used as fertilizer to help replenish the earth for next year's crop. Cooking the juice required 2 or 3 workers to skim out the impurities. The cooking process took about an hour. When the final product was finished, it was poured into cans or jars.

It was common for a family to use 50-75 gallons a year. It was used as a sugar substitute and could be used for making dried apple cake, ginger bread, cookies, and many other desserts.

I would like to thank Jack K. Averitt of Tulsa, Oklahoma, for this information about making molasses.

This recipe was given to me by Wanda McCroskey of Blountville, Tennessee. It won a Blue Ribbon at The Appalachian Fair in 1986. This recipe is over 150 years old.

FLUFFY GINGERBREAD

2 cups flour
1½ tsp. soda
1 tsp. ginger
1 tsp. cinnamon
½ tsp. cloves
½ tsp. salt
¾ cup molasses
2 eggs
1 cup water (boiling)

Mix the spices and salt with flour. Cream butter and sugar together and add eggs one at a time, beating after each addition. Add molasses and mix thoroughly. Add hot water and mix well. Bake in a loaf pan at 350° for about 45 minutes.

Gingerbread is great served with applesauce.

Ginger is a spice from Jamaica, Africa and India. It is available the year around. The Pilgrims brought it from England, and it has always been used in the molasses products. Ginger was here before sugar. What would the molasses be without ginger? What would gingerale be without ginger?

Aunt Lela was the oldest of 8 children when their mother died - the youngest being 5 months old. She never married, and with the help of their father reared the family. She really knew how to live off the land. There was usually 1 single teacher in our 3-teacher school, and that single teacher roomed and boarded at Aunt Lela's for $15 a month which included a bedroom with a wash stand and 3 meals a day. When the 3 youngest children, all girls, where college age, Aunt Lela moved to Denton, Texas, a college town. She rented a boarding house for girls, thus enabling the girls in her familly to go to college. When it was too cold for Marie and me to go home in the buggy, my brother would take us to Aunt Lela's house. She always had something made with molasses. Aunt Lela had a great sense of humor. It must have come in handy during those years. She was also a very creative cook.

AUNT LELA'S MOLASSES CAKE
circa 1920

½ butter
½ cup sugar
1 cup molasses
3 egg yolks
2 cups flour
½ tsp. salt
¼ tsp. allspice
¼ tsp. cloves
1 tsp. cinnamon
½ cup milk,
½ raisins (optional)
2 egg yolks stiffly beaten

Cream butter and sugar. Add egg yolks and molasses and beat well. Mix flour, salt and spices. Add to creamed mixture alternating with milk, raisins and nuts in the last flour mixture. Fold in the stiffly beaten egg whites.

Aunt Lela usually cooked this molasses cake in a large tin biscuit pan without icing, serving it hot with real butter. Sometimes she baked it in 3 layers and iced it with Molasses Mocha Icing.

MOLASSES MOCHA ICING

3 Tbsp. of molasses
3 Tbsp. of top milk (cream
      skimmed off whole milk)
3 tsp. cooled coffee
about 2 cups powdered sugar
nuts chopped fine (enough to
      sprinkle on top

Combine all the ingredients except nuts and sugar. Sift sugar into liquid and beat well. Add enough sugar to make icing the right consistency to spread. Sprinkle with nuts.

MOLASSES PYE
used by my grandmother - Ollie Rogers
this recipe is over 100 years old

3 eggs
1 cup sugar
1 cup molasses
½ cup melted butter
1 tsp. vanilla
1 pie shell (9", unbaked)

Beat molasses until light. Add sugar and beat again. Then add molasses, butter and vanilla. Place in a 9" pie pan. Bake about 10 minutes in a hot oven. Reduce heat by not adding wood. Bake until custard is set.

AUNT LELA'S
ROLLED MOLASSES COOKIES
circa 1920

½ cup butter
1 cup molasses
2½ cups flour
½ tsp. soda
½ tsp. baking soda
1 tsp. grated lemon rind
1 tsp. cinnamon

Put butter and molasses in small sauce pan and bring to a boil. Remove from heat and cool. Combine remaining ingredients and stir in the cooled molasses mixture. Roll dough on lightly floured board to about ¼ inch. Cut with glass. Put on slighjtly greased pan about 2 inches apart. Bake at 350° for 8-10 minutes. It will handle more easily if chilled first in fridge, but Aunt Lela didn't have that luxury.

AUNT LELA'S CHEWY MOLASSES
COOKIES
circa 1920

¾ cup shortening
1 cup sugar
¼ cup molasses
1 egg
2 tsp. soda
2 cups flour

1 Tbsp. hot water
½ tsp cloves
1 tsp. cinnamon
½ tsp. ginger
½ tsp. salt

Cream shortening and sugar, add molasses and egg. Dissolve soda in hot water and add to mixture. Sift together flour and spices, add and mix well. Chill. Form into balls and dip in flour. Place in pan. Bake 375° for 8-10 minutes. Do not over bake. May be used for roll out cookies.

SHOOFLY CAKE
circa 1920

3 cups flour
1 cup shortening
1 cup sugar
1 tsp. soda
1 cup molasses
1 cup hot water

Mix first 3 ingredients until crumbly. Reserve ½ cup crumbs. Mix soda, molasses and 1 cup hot water. Stir in remaining crumbs. Spoon batter into layer cake pan, sprinkle with reserved crumbs. Bake at 350° for 40 minutes. Serve hot.

This recipe was given to me by Gwytha Duncan of Blanchard, Oklahoma. Her grandmother cooked Dried Apple Cakes each Christmas and sent them to friends and gave them to each of her six kids. This recipe is over 50 years old.

DRIED APPLE CAKE

2 cups dried apples (cored
    and chopped fine)
2 cups pure ribbon cane
    molasses

Place chopped apples in colander, wash in slightly warm water and set aside to drain several hours or overnight before cooking. After apples have drained, place into heavy 2 or 3 quart stew pan, add molassas and place over medium heat until mixture begins to bubble. Reduce heat and simmer slowly about 4 hours, stirring well occasionally.

The success or failure of the cake depends on the quality of this finished product. Most of the molasses should be cooked out, if too much is left, cake will be soggy, but if mixture is cooked too fast, apples won't be done and molasses will candy. Making it hard to work into cake and giving cake a scorched flavor. After mixture is cooked to desired doneness, set aside to cool. Before mixture is completely cool, have rest of recipe ready.

1 cup sugar
1 cup butter
3 eggs (separated)
4 cups flour (unsifted)
2 tsp. baking powder
½ tsp. nutmed
½ tsp. allspice
½ tsp. cloves
1 tsp. cinnamon
1 cup buttermilk
1 tsp. soda (mixed into buttermilk)
1 cup unsweetened apple
    sauce
1 cup dromedary pitted dates
    (chopped and floured in
    2 Tbsp. flour)
1 cup pecans (chopped)

Cream together butter and sugar, add beaten egg yolks. Save whites for later. Sift dry ingredients together and add alternating with buttermilk-soda mixture. After ingredients are blended, add warm dried apple and molasses mixture along with applesauce. Mix well. Add dates and pecans, and mix well. Beat egg whites into soft peaks and fold in last. Pour into greased and floured 10" tube pan and bake in slow oven at 250°-275° for 2½ - 3 hours or until knife comes out clean.

Mrs. White died as this book was going to press; she was almost 98 years. old. She has taught me a lot about cooking and living. This recipe is at least 100 years old and has served five generations.

MINNIE WHITE'S
OLD TIMEY TEA CAKES

2 cups sugar
½ tsp. salt
1 tsp. soda
3 tsp. baking powder
1 cup lard
1 cup buttermilk
1 egg
3 cups flour

Put in large crock or use bowl that you use for making biscuits, 3 cups of flour. Make a well in flour. Add salt, soda and baking powder with well-beaten egg to the well. Add lard. Mix with finger tips as you would biscuits. Place on a floured board. Add more flour, if needed to make a dough that you can handle. Roll into ½" pieces and cut into desired size. Bake in a moderately warm oven until slightly brown, being careful not to over cook. In today's oven, it would be 325°.

If you want to fill, mix:
1 cup brown sugar
½ cup white sugar

2 Tbsp. corn syrup
2 Tbsp. butter
⅓ cup heavy cream (today
    we use condensed milk)

Put on stove and heat until sugar is dissolved. Let come to a boil and boil for 3 minutes. Beat until spreading consistency for top of cakes.

FRESH APPLE CAKE
Marie Sumrall
so good!

Mix
1 cup Wesson Oil
2 eggs
3 cups sugar

then add
2½ cups flour
2¼ tsp. baking soda
1 tsp. salt
1 tsp. cinnamon
1 tsp. vanilla
3 cups apples (peeled and diced)

Spread mixture in greased 9"x13" pan. Then sprinkle Butterscotch morsels (6 0z.) and 1/2 cup chopped nuts on top. Bake at 325°- 350° for 40 minutes or until done.

Mrs. Baker was well-known for her fruit cake, even during the Depression Days. I never made it then; we couldn't afford the ingredients. She's been deceased 20 years or more. This is her original recipe.

MRS. BRACH BAKER'S FRUIT CAKE

2 cups brown sugar
2 cups white sugar
1½ cup butter
8 eggs
1½ cups sweet milk
2 cups chopped nuts
1 cup applesauce
1 box raisins (1 lb.)
1 box coconut
1 box currants
15 cent pkg. red hots for trim
1 box dates
3 tsp. vanilla
3 tsp. baking powder
3 tsp. each of nutmeg, clove
    and cinnamon
1 cup wine or grape juice
2 tsp. soda
1 pt. cooked cranberries
about 3 cups flour (enough to
    make stiff batter)

Cream butter, sugar and eggs well. Use part of flour to dredge fruit. Cook cranberries by regular method with water and sugar. Add other ingredients using flour, milk and grapejuice alternating at the end.

Bake in 5 greased 8" cake pans at 350° for about 30 minutes or until brown. To be baked only in layers. Don't ice until cake is cold.

Ice with the following recipe:

MRS. BRACH BAKER'S FRUIT CAKE ICING

2 cups sugar
juice of 2 oranges and 2 lemons
2 cups of boiling water
⅔ cups flour
1 box coconut

Grate the rinds of all lemons and oranges. Put orange and lemon juice and rind in the pan of boiling water and let it come to a boil. Have the sugar and flour mixed together really good and pour in the boiling juice, stirring all the time. Let this come to a boil, then keep at full boil for 3 minutes. Stir until spreading consistency. Add coconut. Spread icing on and between each layer. This will be a soft icing. Decorate with red hots if you so desire.

KITCHEN KAPERS: When storing fruit cake, it's good to put a raw apple or orange peel with the cake for a constant source of moisture. Never serve freshly baked fruit cakes. Store at least 1 week to allow flavors to blend and mellow. Chill before slicing. They will slice more evenly, if chilled.

This recipe was given to me by Cleo Echols. It was enjoyed by her family and friends for many years. She is living near her daughter in Appleton, Wisconsin. Cleo is over 90 years old.

FRESH COCONUT CAKE
Cleo Echols
old

1 cup butter
2 cups sugar
3½ cups flour
3½ tsp. baking powder
1 cup coconut milk, (if not
        enough, finish with sweet
        milk)
8 egg whites (beaten)
½ tsp. vanilla extract
½ tsp. lemon extract

Punch holes in 2 coconut eyes and drain milk to be used in the cake. Bake coconut in 350° oven for 30 minutes. Cool slightly and crack with hammer. Meat will pull away from the shell. Pull off brown skin and grate the fresh coconut for use in cake.

Cream butter and add sugar gradually. Combine flour and baking powder and add flour alternating with coconut milk. Begin with flour and end with flour. Beat egg whites until stiff, but not dry. Fold into creamed mixture. Add flavorings. Bake in 3 floured and greased cake pans at 375° for about 30-35 minutes. Cool before icing.

FRESH COCONUT CAKE ICING

3 cups granulated sugar
1 cup water
2 tsp. vinegar
3 egg whites (beaten)
½ tsp. cream of tartar
1 tsp. lemon extract
1 tsp. vanilla extract

Stir together the sugar, vinegar and water. Cook until it spins a thread. Beat egg whites with cream of tartar. Gradually add sugar mixture to eggs; beat constantly. Add extracts and mix well. Stir in coconut and spread on cooked cake layers. Save some coconut to sprinkle on top and sides of cake.

We always had a fresh coconut at Christmas. We ate a lot of the coconut for snacks just like you would nuts.

KITCHEN KAPERS: To make coconut milk, take the canned coconut and pour an equal amount of milk over the coconut. Let set for 30 minutes. Pour off the liquid and throw away the coconut. You now have a liquid that resembles fresh coconut milk. Use in icings for cakes, coconut pies and candies.

Marietta Madden vows this is the best cake she ever made.

HAWAIIAN CHIFFON CAKE
Marietta Madden

2 cups cake flour (sifted)
1½ cups sugar
3 tsp. baking powder
1 tsp. salt
½ cup salad oil
7 egg yolks (unbeaten)
¾ cup cold water
2 tsp. good vanilla
grated drind of 1 lemon
½ tsp. cream of tartar
7-8 egg whites

Combine dry ingredients in a large mixing bowl. Make a well in center of flour mixture. Pour in the oil, the unbeaten egg yolks, the cold water, vanilla, and lemon rind. Beat until smooth. Whip egg whites until they barely begin to froth. Then add ½ tsp. cream of tartar. Whip until whites form a very stiff peak. Do not under-beat. Pour egg yolk mixture gradually over egg whites, folding until blended - do not stir. Pour into ungreased tube pan. Bake 55 minutes at 325° and increase to 350° for the last 10-15 minutes or until top springs back when touched. Invert pan when done. Coke bottle is good to invert on.

94

HAWAIIAN CHIFFON CAKE
ICING

Cream together
2 Tbsp. shortening
1 Tbsp. butter
½ cup powdered sugar

add alternately
2½ cups powder sugar
½ cup pineapple (drained
and crushed)
Beat until fluffy.

This recipe was told to me by Mrs. White's daughter who lives in Missouri. Mr. White has made this for me and my family, but I never got the recipe. It is good, nourishing and filling, and we always had the ingredients in The Olden Days. I've had lots of calls for this recipe.

MRS. WHITE'S
OLD TIMEY BUTTER ROLLS
This recipe is close to 100 years old.

Make a rich biscuit dough for about 9-10 biscuits. Roll about ½" thick. Spread with lots of butter and cinnamon. Cut as you would any cinnamon roll. Place in baking pan. Cover with about 2 cups milk to which has been added 2 Tbsp. sugar. The baking powder from biscuits will make a porous dough and will thicken the sauce. Cook at 350° until slightly brown. Simple and good.

This cake was made in my kitchen in the middle '50s by a friend, Grace Brooks. She was really a terrific cook and is now deceased. She would caramelize the sugar on Friday and set in the kitchen window and make the cake on Saturday for Sunday dinner.

BURNT SUGAR CAKE

1 cup butter
1½ cups white sugar
3 eggs (separated)
4 Tbsp. caramelized sugar
3 cups cake flour
2 Tbsp. baking powder
½ tsp. salt
1 cup cold water
1 tsp. soda
1 tsp. vanilla

Cream the butter, add the sugar and cream together until the mixture is as light and fluffy as whipped cream. This is very important. Add a small amount of the measured flour to the butter- sugar mixture. Beat the egg yolks until they are thickened and lemon colored. Then add to the butter-sugar mixture. Next add the caramelized sugar syrup, beating again. Sift flour, salt and baking powder together. Now add about ½ cup of flour and beat well. Then add the water in which the soda has been disolved. Continue adding alternately the flour and liquid until all is used. Add the vanilla. Beat a few strokes after each addition. Do not overbeat because this makes a dry stiff cake. Fold in stiffly beaten egg whites and turn into layer pans which have been lined with oiled wax paper. I like to use a long pan about 9"x5"x2". Bake for 30 minutes at 380°. Cool on a wire rack and ice with Burnt Sugar Icing.

BURNT SUGAR ICING

2 cups sugar
2 Tbsp. butter
½ cup milk
¼ cup boiling water
⅛ tsp. salt
1 tsp. vanilla

Caramelize ½ cup of the sugar. Add boiling water. Stir until dissolved. Add butter, milk, salt, and the remainer of the sugar. Boil to soft ball stage. Cool to room temperature. Add flavoring. Beat until thick and creamy.

Burnt sugar was used by our pioneer predecessors. It furnished a different flavor when flavorings were hard to find. It would keep indefinitely when caramelized and was often used for syrup on hot bread. The pioneers used an iron-like skillet with about 4-5 legs that kept the vessel away from the open fire (fireplace). The women crossing the prairie could have burnt sugar in limited amounts, I'm sure.

See "How To Caramelize Sugar" on page 122.

GEORGIA PEACH SHORTCAKE

4 large ripe peaches
3 cups flour (sifted)
4 tsp. baking powder
1 tsp. salt
1 tsp. cinnamon
½ cup brown sugar (packed)
¾ cup margarine
½ cup pecan pieces
1 egg
¾ cup milk
sugar to sweeten peaches
1 cup heavy cream (whipped)
¼ tsp. almond flavoring

Peel and slice peaches. Sift flour, baking powder, salt, and cinnamon into a large bowl and stir in brown sugar. Cut in margarine with pastry blender until crumbly. Stir in pecans. Beat eggs slightly with milk. Add all at once to flour mixture. Stir with fork until blended. Spread dough on 2 (9") pans to within ½ inch of edge. Bake 400° for 20-25 minutes or until golden. Sweeten peaches to taste. Put flavor in whipped cream. Place 1 shortcake layer on serving plate. Top with peaches and whip cream. Add remaining shortcake layer. Spoon remaining peaches and whip cream over top layer. Yields 6 servings.

STRAWBERRY NUT SHORTCAKE

½ cup sour cream
⅓ cup shortening
1 egg
½ cup walnuts or pecan pieces
1½ cups flour
¼ cup sugar
¼ tsp. soda
1 tsp. baking powder
½ tsp. salt
1 quart strawberries
1 cup whipping cream
        (whipped)

Combine sour cream, shortening and egg, beat until smooth. Add nuts. Sift dry ingredients together; add sour cream mixture. Stir just enough to moisten. Drop by ⅓ cup portions onto greased baking sheet. Bake for 400° for 12-14 minutes. Split shortcake. Spoon strawberries and whip cream over half the shortcakes, top with remaining shortcakes. Top with remaining strawberries and whip cream. Yields 6 servings.

This cake has been around for several years. I don't know the origin, but it was thought to have been used first in school cafeterias. Beets provide protein in diet. Try it, I think you'll like it.

BEETNIK CAKE

1 cup butter
2 cups sugar
2 eggs
2 cups raisins
½ tsp. salt
2 tsp. cinnamon
3½ cups flour
2 tsp. soda
4 Tbsp. cocoa
2 cups hot beets (blended to the consistency of apple sauce)
1 cup nuts

Cream butter. beat in sugar. Add eggs and mix well. Stir in raisins. Dredge in some of the flour. Sift dry ingredients together. Stir into butter mixture. Stir in nuts and beets. Pour into 2 greased loaf pans. Bake at 350° for 1 hour. Ice with favorite chocolate icing.

KITCHEN KAPERS: Drain a can of whole or sliced beets. Save the juice from sweet pickles and marinate the beets for a few days. Guess what you've got? Some pickled beets for a fraction of the cost, not to mention the labor saved.

BLACK WALNUT CAKE
Juarine Wooldridge
(a friend from Missouri)

⅔ cups butter
1½ cups sugar
1 tsp. vanilla
3 egg yokes (beaten)
3 egg whites (beaten)
2 cups flour
2½ tsp. baking powder
¾ cup milk
1 cup ground black walnuts

Cream butter, sugar and vanilla until fluffy. Add beaten egg yolks and beat thoroughly. Add dry ingredients alternating with milk, beginning and ending with flour. Add nuts and fold in stiffly beaten egg whites. Place batter in 2 greased 9" pans. Bake at 350° for about 30 minutes. When cool, frost with Black Walnut Frosting.

black walnut cake frosting

2 cups light brown sugar
½ cup water
½ cup light corn syrup
2 egg whites (stiffly beaten)
black walnuts (finely ground)

Cook over medium heat sugar, water, syrup until it spins a thread. Pour syrup over beaten egg whites until of spreading consistency. Spread between layers , on top and sides of cake. Sprinkle black walnuts on top.

KENTUCKY BOURBON CAKE

3 sticks margarine (room temperature
2 cups sugar
6 eggs (room temperature)
½ cup molasses
4 cups flour
2 tsp. baking powder
2 tsp. nutmeg

chop
1 cup candied pineapple
1 cup candied cherries
1 cup orange marmalade
2 cups chopped pecans
1½ cup bourbon

Cream butter and sugar. Add eggs; one at a time. Beat well after each addition. Add baking powder and nutmeg to flour. Put fruit and marmalade in large bowl. Dredge fruit and marmalode with 1 cup of the flour mixture. Mix remainder of creamed mixture alternating with bourbon. Stir in fruits and nuts. Grease 2 large loaf pans, lined with greased heavy brown paper. Spoon batter into pans and cover with greased brown paper. Bake at 250° for 2½ to 3 hours until toothpicks come out clean. To ripen the cake, wrap in cloth dampened in bourbon. Place in tin container with raw apple slices arranged around the cake. Ready to serve in about a month.

This is a large cake which made it a very popular Christmas cake. The ingredients were in every kitchen. We might not have candied citrus, but we all had watermellon rind preserves and blackberry jam.

AUNT BURNICE'S WATERMELLON RIND PRESERVE CAKE
circa 1920

3 cups sifted flour
1 tsp. soda
¼ tsp. salt
1 tsp. each allspice, clove, cinammon, nutmeg
1 cup of chopped and drained watermellon rind preserves
1 cup butter
1½ cups sugar
3 eggs well-beaten
1 cup blackberry jam
1 cup buttermilk

Sift together flour, soda, salt, and spices. Use a little of the flour mixture over the nuts and citrus to coat. Cream butter until soft and smooth. Gradually add sugar and beat until light and fluffy. Beat in eggs and jam. Add flour mixture alternating with milk - beginning and ending with flour. Beat until smooth after each addition. Bake in 3 layer pans at 350° for 20-25 minutes. Frost, if desired, with fluffy white frosting.

MRS. MILLS OLD-FASHIONED POUND CAKE
circa 1900

2 cups flour
1 cup butter
1⅔ cups sifted granulated sugar
5 eggs
1 tsp. vanilla

Sift flour, measure and sift again 5 more times. Cream buter, add sugar and beat.until you no longer can see sugar grains. Then add 1 egg and beat until no egg can be seen. Proceed as before, and when the last egg has been added, beat long and hard. Add the flour and beat again. When it becomes a creamy mass, add vanilla. Bake in a greased and floured stem pan. If a stem pan is not available, grease and flour a glass. Put glass in the center of a 9"-10" pan and pour batter around the glass. Put in a 275° oven for 1 hour or until done. Pound cakes were never glazed or iced. It will keep really good, if you hide it.

MRS. MILLS' SPONGE CAKE
circa 1910

4 large or 5 small eggs
1 cup fine granulated sugar
1 cup sifted pastry flour
grated rind and juice of ½ lemon

Beat yolks until creamy and thick. Add sugar and beat until light in color. Add lemon. Beat egg whites until stiff and nearly dry. Fold them in with care; so not to break down the air bubbles. Sift in flour lightly and fold over. Cook in moderate oven at 350° for 40-50 minutes. If mixed and baked properly, you will look far to find a better sponge cake than this one.

This recipe is from Mrs. Mills' book of pasted recipes that her daughter-in-law, Marie Mills, has in her possession.

BUTTERMILK WHITE CAKE
circa 1910

2½ cups sifted cake flour
1½ cups sugar
1 tsp. salt
1 tsp. soda
1 tsp. baking powder
¼ cup butter or oleo
¼ cup shortening
1½ tsp. vanilla
½ cup buttermilk
4 egg whites

Sift together dry ingredients into a large mixing bowl. Add butter, shortening, vanilla, and ¾ cup buttermilk. Beat 3 minutes at medium speed on electric mixer. Add remaining buttermilk and egg whites. Beat 2 minutes longer. Bake in 2 greased and floured 8" cake pans at 350° for 30-35 minutes. Cool and frost with 7 minute frosting.

I've had lots of calls for this recipe.

BUTTER RUM CAKE
in memory of Amy Thaggard

2 cups sifted flour
1¾ cups sugar
5 eggs
½ lb. of margarine
1 tsp. good vanilla
1 tsp. butter flavor
1 tsp. rum flavor

Cream margarine thoroughly. Add sugar gradually, and add eggs one at at time. Mix well after each addition. Add extracts. Next add flour a little at a time and blend well. Pour batter in a greased and dusted 10" stem pan. Bake in a 350° oven for about an hour or unitl a tooth pick inserted in center comes out clean.

BUTTER RUM CAKE ICING

1 cup sugar
½ cup water
1 tsp. vanilla
1 tsp. rum flavor

Bring sugar and water to a boil. Cool and add rum flavor and vanilla. Use pastry brush and apply to warm cake.

POTATO CAKE
in memory of
Lessie Kate Austin Hickman
this recipe has been used for 4 generations

1 cup butter
2 cups sugar
2 tsp. baking powder
½ cup milk
4 eggs
2¼ cup flour
1 cup mashed Irish potatoes
2 tsp. cloves
1 tsp. each of allspice and
      nutmeg
1 tsp. cinnamon
2 tsp. cocoa
1½ cups nuts
1 cup raisins
1 cup dates

Mix in order given. Bake in an angel food cake pan at 350° for about an hour. When cool, wrap and store in a cool place. Flavor and moistness improve with age. Especially good for holiday season.

Lessie Hickman's father was an early automobile dealer in our area, which probably made her very popular. She was the only girl in a big family of boys. One Friday night her father allowed her to drive the entire football team to an out-of-town game in her touring car. I'm sure some of the team had to ride on the running boards. Four questions come to mind. How many players on the team? How much equipment did they have? How cold was it that night? Was her dad crazy to let her go? Lessie was the first "Miss Altus."

AUNT LELA'S
SWEET POTATO CAKE

½ cups cooking oil
2 cups sugar
4 eggs (separated)
4 Tbsp. hot water
2½ cups cake flour
3 tsp. baking powder
1 tsp. cinnamon
1 tsp. nutmeg
1½ cups raw grated sweet
    potatoes
1 cup chopped nuts
1 tsp. vanilla

Combine cooking oil and sugar and beat until smooth. Add egg yolks and beat well. Add hot water, then dry ingredients which have been sifted together. Stir in nuts, potatoes and vanilla and beat well. Beat egg whites until stiff and fold into mixture. Bake in 3 layers in a 350° oven for 25-30 minutes. Cool and frost with Sweet Chocolate Filling.

I have added this icing to Aunt Lela's original recipe.

SWEET CHOCOLATE FILLING

⅓ cup butter or margarine
⅔ cup evaporated milk
⅓ tsp. salt
3 cups powdered sugar
1 (6 oz.) package of semi-
    sweet chocolate chips

Combine butter of margarine, milk and salt in a sauce pan. Bring to a boiling point, stirring constantly. Remove from heat, add the chocolate pieces, stirring until smooth. Then gradually beat in the powder sugar until thick enough to spread.

FLUFFY WHITE FROSTING
an easy version of Seven Minute Icing

1½ cup granulated sugar
½ cup water
½ tsp. cream of tartar
a pinch of salt
3 unbeaten egg whites
1 tsp. vanilla

Combine sugar, water, cream of tartar, and salt in saucepan. Bring to boiling point. Stir until sugar is idssolved. Very slowly add unbeaten egg whites to the sugar mixture, beating constantly with electric mixer until stiff peaks form. Beat in vanilla. Enough to frost 3 layers.

This recipe was given to Helen Byrd by her mother, Minnie Pearl Griffis. It was dated "1960," and a note saying that she had used it every Christmas since 1912.

JAM CAKE
in memory of Minnie Pearl Griffis

2 cups sugar
⅔ cup butter
1 cup buttermilk
1 tsp. soda
1 tsp. of each spice: cinnamon,
        nutmeg, allspice
1 lb. raisins
3 eggs
4 cups flour
1 cup nuts
1 cup blackberry jam or jam of
        your choice

Mix as you would any cake. Dredge nuts in part of flour. Bake in moderate oven in 2 layers 25-30 minutes.

Ice with favorite icing.
Minnie would use:

2 cups sugar
1 cup butter
½ cup cream

Boil until thick and beat until spreading consistency. If it gets too thick, add a little cream.

This recipe dates back prior to World War II. It certainly couldn't be made during the War, because it calls for too much sugar and candy. Both were scarce.

CANDY BAR CAKE

2 sticks margarine
2 cups sugar
4 eggs
8 (5 cent) Hershey chocolate
    bars or Milky Way bars
½ tsp. soda
1 cup buttermilk
2½ cups flour,
2 tsp. vanilla
⅛ tsp. salt
1 cup pecans (broken)

Cream butter and sugar. Add eggs one at a time, beating after each. Melt chocolate bars and add to egg mixture. Add soda to buttermilk and fold in flour alternating beginning and ending with flour. Stir in vanilla, salt and nuts. Bake in 10" stem pan at 325° for 90 minutes or until done.

All dried fruit was sold from a wooden box that was lined with paper similar to wax paper. You dug them out with your fingers, if you didn't buy the whole crate. They were place in a paper bag, folded over from the top, and tied with a string.

The strings were never discarted. You might wrap a sore toe or finger with a clean white rag and tie it with a string. My brother often made balls from the twine string by taking some rubber from a discarded inner-tube; wrapping the string around it until it was the right size to play baseball or anti-over. When the string got loose on the ball, he just wrapped more string over it.

MY MOTHER'S SOUR CREAM PRUNE CAKE
in memory of LaVerne Jackson

1½ cups brown sugar
1 cup thick sour cream
¼ cup cold water
2 eggs (well-beaten)
½ tsp. soda
½ tsp. salt
1½ cups flour
1 cup uncooked prunes (pitted)
2 tsp. baking powder
1 tsp. cinnamon
1 tsp. cloves
1 tsp. nutmeg

Combine eggs, sugar, sour cream, and water. Mix well. Sift together 1¼ cups flour with baking soda, salt, and spices. Adds alternating with flour and first mixture, beginning and ending with flour. Beat thoroughly. Add prunes that have been cut into small pieces and dredged in ¼ cup of the flour. Cook in stem pan in a 350° oven for about 50-60 minutes. So good hot with that big bowl of freshly churned butter that always set in the center of the table.

MARIE MILLS' BROWNIES
35 year old recipe, easy to make

Grease well a 9" square pan

Sift together in a 2 quart mixing bowl
¾ cup flour (sifted)
1¼ cups sugar
½ cup cocoa
⅓ cup instant dry milk
¼ tsp. salt

Add all at once
½ cup soft shortening
1 egg (unbeaten)
¼ cup water
1 tsp. vanilla
¼ cup nuts

Mix until blended, then stir really hard for a minute. Add ½ cup nuts. Spread batter in greased pan. Bake for 30 minutes in a 350° oven or until cake pulls away from side of pan. Cool about 30 minutes before cutting. Will stay nice and moist if you cover pan right out of the oven. That won't be necessary, because it want last long enough to bother.

CRANBERRY CAKE
in memory of Este McCall

3 eggs (separated)
2 cups sugar
½ cup boiling water
1 cup sifted flour
2 tsp. baking powder
½ tsp. soda
a pinch of salt
½ lb. cranberries (1 cup)
½ cup butter
1 cup light cream
light rum to taste

Beat egg yolks and 1 cup of sugar with rotary beater until light. Stir flour, baking powder and salt together. Add to egg yolk mixture. Beat until smooth. Add cranberries. Beat egg whites until smooth; fold into butter. Turn into greased and floured 8" square pan. Bake at 375° for 30-40 minutes or until done.

Combine cream, butter, cream, and remaining sugar in saucepan. Bring to boil over low heat, stirring until smooth. Remove from heat; add rum. Cut into 8 squares. Serve hot sauce over cake

Lou Allen's Applesauce Cake was made with her home-canned apples (mashed). Sometimes she used canned peaches that she had mashed with a fork. Either fruit for this recipe is a good choice.

LOU ALLEN'S APPLESAUCE CAKE
at least 70 years old

½ cup margarine or butter
1½ cups thick applesauce
1 tsp. soda
1¼ cup sugar
4 eggs (well beaten)
½ cup sour milk
2½ cups flour
1 tsp. cinnamon
1 tsp. nutmeg
½ tsp. allspice
½ tsp. salt

Cream margarine and sugar. Add eggs and applesauce. Beat thoroughly. Mix flour, baking soda, salt and spices. Add alternating with milk and first ingredients, beginning and ending with flour. Beat thoroughly. Bake in greased stem pan in a 350° oven for 50-60 minutes.

KITCHEN KAPERS: To make the best applesauce, quarter desired amount of apples. Cook in a heavy saucepan with a tightly closed lid without water. Do not peel apples. When tender run through a ricer. No sugar will be needed, if any - very little. It will be a pretty color - tinge of red.

This was a recipe we could use before the tomatoes were ripe.

GREEN TOMATO CAKE

2 cups sugar
¾ cup butter
3 eggs
2 cups green tomatoes (finely
        chopped)
1 cup pecans (chopped)
        walnuts may be used
2 tsp. vanilla
2 tsp. orange extract
½ cup cocoa
2½ cups flour
2½ tsp. baking soda
1 tsp. salt or less
1 tsp. cinnamon
½ cup milk

Cream butter and sugar. Add the eggs one at a time. Beat well after each addition. Blend in the green tomatoes. Add nuts and flavorings. Combine dry ingredients and add alternating with the milk, beginning and ending with flour. Pour into a greased tube pan. Bake in 350° oven for about 1 hour. Frost, if desired.

KITCHEN KAPERS: To peel tomatoes easily, hold over a flame for a few seconds, and they can be peeled with a knife in a short time.

I don't know the history of this cake. It's been around a long time and was a very popular cake at least 45 years ago.

DR. BYRD CAKE

3 cups sifted flour
2 cups sugar
3 eggs
1 tsp. baking soda
1 tsp. cinnamon
1 tsp. salt
1½ tsp. vanilla
1 (8 oz.) can crushed pineapple
        (undrained)
1½ cups vegetable oil
2 cups bananas (mashed)

Sift all dry ingredients together. Add bananas, oil, eggs, vanilla, and pineapple to dry ingredients. Stir to blend. Do not beat. Pour into greased stem pan. Bake about 1 hour in a 350° oven. Cool before removing from pan. Sometimes, I add ½ cup coconut to the batter.

It's very good iced with

½ cup margarine
1 (4 oz.) package cream cheese
½ box powdered sugar
1 tsp. vanilla

Mix all ingredients well and spread on cooled cake.

This cake became popular in the late '40s and early '50s. These cakes were rarely frosted.

LEMON CHIFFON CAKE
in memory of Maude Ellington

2 cups flour
1⅓ cups sugar
3 tsp. baking powder
1 tsp. salt
½ cup cooking oil
¾ cup water
1 Tbsp. grated lemon peel
7 egg yolks (unbeaten)
½ tsp. cream of tartar
7 egg whites (beaten)

Combine dry ingredients in a large mixing bowl. Make a well in the center of flour mixture. Pour in the oil, lemon peel and egg yolks. Beat until smooth. In another large bowl, add cream of tartar to egg whites. Beat whites until they form a very stiff peak when raised by the beater. Gradually pour egg yolk mixture over the beaten whites, folding with rubber scrapper until just blended. Pour into an ungreased 10" tube pan. Bake at 350° for about 55 minutes. A bottle is good to invert the pan on, so it can air cool. When cake is cold, loosen edges with spatula.

KITCHEN KAPERS: Before grating lemon or oranges, dip the grater in cold water. The peel will come off more easily.

CAKE THAT DOESN'T LAST
Marie Sumrall
she is in her mid-eighties in age

2 cups flour
1 tsp. soda
3 eggs (beaten)
1 cup cooking oil
2 cups sugar
1 tsp. salt
1 cup nuts (chopped)
2 cups bananas (mashed)
1 (8 oz.) can pineapple
      crushed (drained)
1 tsp. black walnut extract
1 tsp. vanilla

Put all ingredients in a big bowl. Stir to mix. Do not beat or whip. Bake in a bundt tube pan or loaf pan at 350° for about 60-75 minutes.

"A fool's wrath is presently known:
but a prudent man covereth shame."
Proverbs 11:16

MISSISSIPPI MUD CAKE

2 sticks oleo
3 cups sugar
3 Tbsp. cocoa
4 eggs
1½ cups flour
1 tsp. vanilla
1½ cup coconut
1½ cups chopped nuts (optional)
1 (7 oz.) pkg. of marshmallows

Cream sugar, oleo and cocoa. Add eggs and vanilla and mix well. Add coconut, nuts and flour. Beat 2 minutes. Bake in well-greased 15"x19" pan for 30-40 minutes at 350° oven. When cake is done and still hot, spread the top with marshmallow cream while in pan. Let cool and ice with frosting made with:

1 stick oleo
4 tsp. cocoa
6 Tbsp. milk
1 lb. powdered sugar

Add vanilla. Mix well and spread over cake.

KITCHEN KAPERS: Do not chop or grind nuts. You'll lose flavor and some of their natural oil.

CUSTARD PIE
Diane Messenger
Bellevue, Michigan

This is poured into a pie pan and makes a thin crust on bottom. Best with whole milk or part cream.

4 eggs
⅔ cup sugar
⅛ tsp. salt
½ tsp. nutmeg
½ tsp. cinnamon
2 cups milk
2 heaping Tbsp. flour.

Beat eggs, add sugar, salt, spice, and flour. Add milk. Bake in a 375° oven for 30 minutes.

BUTTERMILK COCONUT PIE
Diane Messenger
Bellevue, Michigan

3 eggs - beat and add
1½ cup sugar
½ cup oleo (melted)
1⅓ cup flaked coconut
⅓ cup buttermilk
1 tsp. vanilla

Pour into unbaked pie crust. Bake at 350° for 1 hour.

KITCHEN KAPERS: When making pies that you bake in crust, take a white of an egg and float it all around the crust. Remove and use in another way. This will prevent a soggy crust.

HOW TO CARAMELIZE SUGAR

Put one cup of grandulated sugar into a heavy skillet. An iron one is better. Heat it over low heat until sugar melts. Be careful not to let it burn. When all the sugar is melted and is about the color of brown syrup, remove from heat and allow it to cool slightly before adding ½ cup of hot water. Be sure and stand back when adding the water, because the mixture will steam and splatter. As soon as the sugar has dissolved, let it cook for 3 or 4 minutes more.

This will make about 1 cup of thick caramelized syrup and will keep indefinitely.

Use what your recipes calls for. Use for cakes, pies, sauces, pudding, or ice cream.

SAUCES AND FROSTINGS FOR DESSERTS

SEVEN MINUTE ICING
good to frost 10" tube cake or 2 layer cake

2 cups sugar
1 Tbsp. light corn syrup
⅛ Tbsp. salt
½ cup water
2 egg whites
1 tsp. vanilla

Mix in small saucepan the sugar, syrup, salt; stir over fire until sugar is dissolved. Boil until it forms a soft ball if a little is dropped in cold water. Beat the egg whites with a rotary beater until nearly stiff. Add the syrup in a thin steady stream into egg whites. Beat constantly until it is smooth, glossy and of spreading consistency. Beat in vanilla and spread immediately.

ORANGE FROSTING
good for stem cake or 2 layer cake

4 Tbsp. orange juice (concentrated)
2 cups powdered sugar (sifted)
1 tsp. lemon juice
2 Tbsp. butter (soft)

Put all ingredients in mixing bowl. Beat 5 minutes with electric beater. The long beating lessens the taste of the uncooked frosting. Add more sugar if you need a thicker and smoother spreading consistency.

SWEET WHIPPED CREAM

1 cup whipping cream
6 Tbsp. powdered sugar (sifted)
1 tsp. vanilla

Whip cream until stiff. Fold in sugar and vanilla.

CHOCOLATE SAUCE
good on puddings or ice cream

4 squares bitter chocolate
1 cup granulaed sugar
1 cup brown sugar (packed)
1 cup boiling water
3 Tbsp. butter
1 tsp. vanilla

Melt the chocolate in top of double boiler. Put the sugar in a small sauce pan and add the hot water. Stir until sugar is dissolved. Remove the melted chocolate from heat and stir in the sweet water. Whisk until well-blended. Boil for 2 minutes. Remove from heat; stir in butter and vanilla. Cool before using. If refrigerated will keep several weeks.

BUTTERSCOTCH SAUCE
good on puddings and ice cream

⅔ cup light corn syrup
1½ cups light brown sugar
4 Tbsp. butter
1 tsp. vanilla
1 cup heavy cream

Combine with sugar, syrup, butter and boil about 10 minutes. It should be quite thick. Remove from heat and add vanilla. Cool and stir in vanilla. Cool. Good on puddings. This will keep good when refrigerated. Good on ice cream.

124

HARD SAUCE
good on bread pudding

½ cup butter (room temperature)
1½ -2 cups powdered sugar
⅛ tsp. nutmeg
2 tsp. rum, brandy or sherry

Beat the butter and 1 cup of sugar with electric beater until well-blended. Add the nutmeg and flavoring and enough additional sugar to make a frim paste. Put in a small bowl or decorated mold and chill. Dust slightly with nutmeg when you serve it. Apple juice can be substituted for brandy.

APRICOT SAUCE
good on bread pudding

1 cup apricot juice
1 cup apricots (chopped and
        cooked)
1 Tbsp. flour or cornstarch
⅓ cup sugar
1 Tbsp. butter

Combine flour with sugar. Add apricot juice. Mix until smooth. Cook in thick saucepan, stirring constantly until thick. Add apricots and butter. Cook until flavors are blended.

FRESH COCONUT PIE

This pie is so good; it's worth the effort.

1¼ cups milk
1 cup grated fresh coconut
    (well-packed)
2 eggs (separated)
⅔ cup sugar
1 tsp. cornstarch
1 envelope gelatin (unflavored)
a pinch of salt
1 cup cream (whipped)
½ cup coconut (flaked and
        toasted)
9-10" pie shell
1 tsp. vanilla

Heat milk to scalding, pour over coconut and let stand for about an 1 hour. Put through a fine wire strainer, pressing to extract all the liquid. Discard the coconut. Beat egg yolks, slightly, then beat in the coconut flavored milk. In a pan, mix sugar, cornstarch, gelatin and salt. Blend in egg/milk mixture. Cook over low heat, stirring until thickened. Chill. When set, beat with electric mixer, fold in whip cream and vanilla. Fold in egg whites that have been beaten until firm. Pour into pie shell and chill for several hours. Garnish top with toasted coconut.

APPLE SPONGE PIE
This is a deep dish pie.

Line a deep dish pie pan with a rich crust. Flute the edge so it will stand high over the pan. Fill with this custard.

3 eggs (separated)
½ cup sugar
2 Tbsp. flour
¼ tsp. nutmeg
1¼ cup milk
2 cups sweetened applesauce
1 Tbsp. lemon juice

Beat the egg yolks. Stir the flour and sugar together. Then add the nutmeg and milk. Mix thoroughly and add the slightly sweetened applesauce with the lemon juice. Fold into the applesauce mixture the stiffly beaten egg whites. Put into the pastry-lined deep pan. Bake until firm. The custard should never boil. Put in 450° oven for 10 minutes until crust is set; then lower to 325°. Continue to bake for 30 minutes until custard is set. Be sure to use a tart apple for your sauce. You will be cooking this recipe often.

KITCHEN KAPERS: When using ovenglass baking pans, always lower temperature by 25°.

Mettie Hunter's Date Pie was always requested by her daughter, Dicey, for Christmas dinner.

DATE PIE
Mettie Hunter

12 dates (chopped)
1 cup cream
1 Tbsp. flour
¾ cup sugar
2 egg yolks

Mix flour and sugar. Combined with cream. Cook over direct heat, stirring constantly until thick. Add beaten egg yolks and cook 2 more minutes longer. Add dates to hot mixture. Add nuts, if desired. Cool and pour in baked shell.

PINTO BEAN PIE
a good way to use left-over beans

2 cups pinto beans (cooked)
2 cups sugar
2 Tbsp. flour
½ cup margarine (melted)
4 eggs
1 tsp. vanilla
1 tsp. nutmeg
2 (8") uncooked pie shell

Place beans in large mixing bowl; mash until smooth. Stir in sugar, flour and margarine. Beat in eggs one at a time. Add nutmeg and vanilla. Mix well. Spoon bean mixture into pastry shells. Bake at 350° for 35 minutes until browned. Serve warm. Top with whipped cream or dessert topping, if desired.

SOUTHERN CHOCOLATE-PECAN PIE

1 (4 oz.) package sweet cooking
    chocolate
¼ cup butter
1⅔ cup evaporated milk
1½ cup sugar
3 Tbsp. cornstarch
⅛ tsp. salt
2 eggs
1 tsp. vanilla
1 (10") uncooked pie shell
1⅓ cup coconut (flaked)
1½ cup pecans (chopped)

Mix chocolate and butter in saucepan. Place over low heat, stirring constantly, until blended. Remove from heat; blend in the evaporated milk gradually; pour into pie shell. Combine coconut and pecans and sprinkle over filling. Bake at 375° for 40-50 minutes or until puffed and browned. Cover loosely with aluminum foil during last 10 minutes of baking, if topping browns too quickly. Cool at least for 4 hours. Filling will set while cooking. It can be garnished with dollops of prepared whipped topping. Serves 8-10.

VANILLA CREAM PIE
A basic cream pie that has several variations.

¾ sugar
3 Tbsp. cornstarch
3 eggs yolks (beaten)
¼ tsp. salt
2 cups milk
2 Tbsp. butter
1 tsp. vanilla
1 (9") pie shell

Combine sugar, flour and salt. Gradually add 2 cups milk. Mix well. Cook and stir over medium heat until mixture thickens and boils. Cook 2 more minutes. Remove from heat. Stir small amount of hot mixture into 3 beaten egg yolks. Immediately return to hot mixture. Cook 2 minutes longer, stirring constantly. Remove from heat. Add 2 Tbsp. butter and 1 tsp. vanilla. Pour into cooled baked 9" pie shell. Spread 1 recipe meringue (3 egg whites) atop pie and bake at 350° for 12-15 minutes. If you prefer whipped cream, cover with waxed paper or plastic wrap, touching the entire surface of hot pie to prevent skim from forming on surface of filling in crust.

See meringue recipe on page 138.

KITCHEN KAPERS: Cornstarch has almost twice the thickening power of flour. Allow 2 Tbsp. of cornstarch for each cup of milk. Mix in a little cold water and then stir in hot mixture and cook for about 15 minutes. This will insure a cooked taste rather than a raw taste. 1 egg will equal ½ Tbsp. of constarch.

CREAM PIE VARIATIONS

CHOCOLATE CREAM PIE

Prepare vanilla cream pie. Increase sugar to 1 cup. Chop 2 (1 oz.) unsweetened chocolate. Add the milk. Top with meringue and bake as directed.

COCONUT CREAM PIE

For a luscious coconut cream pie, add 1 cup flaked coconut to vanilla cream pie filling. Top with meringue (3 egg whites). Sprinkle with ½ cup coconut and bake as directed.

BANANA CREAM PIE

Slice 3 bananas into cooled pie crust. Top with vanilla cream pie filling and meringue (3 egg whites). Bake as directed.

BUTTERSCOTCH CREAM PIE

Substitute brown sugar for granulated sugar. Increase butter to 3 Tbsp.. Top with meringue (3 egg whites). Bake as directed.

PINEAPPLE CREAM PIE

Drain juice from a medium size can of crushed pineapple in a measuring cup. Finish with milk to make 2 cups liquid. Add pineapple to cream filling. Fill crust. Bake and add meringue.

131

I had never heard of Sugar Pie, until I showed my first cook-book in Nashville, Tennessee. I never found it in Oklahoma. I had to come to Tennesse to find it. A lot of folks have requested this recipe.

SUGAR PIE

3 eggs (beaten)
5 Tbsp. sugar
3 Tbsp. flour
a pinch of salt
½ tsp. nutmeg
1 tsp. cinnamon
½ tsp. vanilla
2 cups milk

Mix flour and sugar together. Add eggs to milk. Stir in flavoring. After mixing, pour in unbacked shell. Sprinkle a little nutmeg on top and dot with 3 or 4 pats of butter. Start crust at 450° for 10-12 minutes. Reduce heat to 325° and bake for 30-40 minutes.

EGG NOG PIE
in memory of Effie Talley
just uses flavorings

4 eggs (separated)
½ cup sugar
½ tsp. salt
½ cup warm water
¼ cup cold water
1 envelope of gelatin
½ cup sugar
1 tsp. nutmeg
2 tsp. rum or bourbon flavoring
heavy cream (optional)

Combine the slightly beaten egg yolks, ½ cup sugar, salt, and warm water. Set them over boiling water, stirring constantly, and cook until mixture coats a spoon. Soften the gelatin in the cold water and add to the hot custard, stirring until it is dissolved. Set aside to cool. When the mixture starts to congeal, fold in the stiffly beaten egg whites, which have been blended with the additional sugar, nutmeg and flavoring. Pour the mixture into a 9" baked pie shell and chill until firm. You may spread it with a layer of whipped cream, sprinkled with nutmeg before serving, but it is delicious without it.

HOOD'S PECAN PIE
Louelyn Hood
Hokes Bluff. Alabama

1½ cups pecans (broken)
5 eggs (beaten)
¾ cup sugar
½ stick oleo (melted)
1 bottle Karo syrup (Green
        label, maple flavor)

Makes 2 pies. Sprinkle pecans in 2 unbaked pie shells. Pour over this, the mixture of well-beaten eggs, sugar, Karo syrup, and Oleo. Bake at 350° for 45 minutes.

This recipe by Juanita Fails was given to me by her daughter, Sue Henry. Debbie Henry, a granddaughter, now makes this pie.

PUMPKIN CHIFFON PIE
in memory of Juanita Fails

2½ cups pumpkin
2 cups milk
1½ cup sugar
2 Tbsp. sorghum
3 eggs
½ cup flour
½ tsp. salt
1 tsp. cinnamon
¼ tsp. each of nutmeg, cloves,
    ginger, allspice
2 Tbsp. butter (melted)

Beat egg yolks. Add sugar, sorghum, melted butter, and milk. Sift flour with spices. To first mixture, add pumpkin. Then stir in dry ingredients. Pour into a double boiler and cook slowly until quite thick. While still hot, fold in stiffly beaten egg whites. Pour mixture into freshly baked shells. Serve with whipped cream. Recipe makes 3 small pies or 2 large ones. May keep in refrigerator for several days.

KITCHEN KAPERS: For best resultss when whipping cream, put the bowl and whisk in the refrigerator for 30 minutes.

PUMPKIN PECAN PIE
really different

for pumpkin layer
1 egg (lightly beaten)
1 cup pumpkin (from solid
      pack can)
⅓ cup granulated sugar
1 tsp. pumpkin pie spice
1 (9") unbaked pie shell (4 cup
      volume)

for pecan layer
⅔ cup light corn syrup
2 eggs (lightly beaten)
½ cup grandulated sugar
3 Tbsp. butter or margarine
      (melted)
½ tsp. vanilla extract
1 cup pecan halves

For pumpkin layer, combine egg, pumpkin, sugar and pie spice in medium bowl. Spread over bottom of pie shell.

For pecan layer, combine corn syrup, eggs, sugar, butter and vanilla in same bowl. Stir in pecans. Spoon over pumpkin layer. Bake in a pre-heated 350° oven for 50 minutes or until filling is set. Cool on a wire rack.

KENTUCKY APPLE STACK CAKE

Ruby Mae Reed
Tulsa, Oklahoma

¾ cup shortening or butter
1 cup sugar
1 cup molasses
1 cup buttermilk
4 cups flour (all purpose)
3 eggs
1 tsp. baking soda
½ tsp. salt
2 tsp. baking powder
½ tsp. each cinnamon and
    cloves or allspice and
    nutmeg
3 cups thick applesauce
    (made from dried apples
    if available)
lemon or vanilla extract

Make applesauce sweetened and spiced. Cream shortening and sugar. Blend well. Blend in molasses and mix well. Add eggs one at a time. Mix well after each egg. Add milk alternately with sifted dry ingredients. Mix will be stiff. Divide into 6 balls. Place each one in 8" cakepans. Bake 350° for 18 minutes. When cool, stack in layers with apples in between layers. Can be iced with favorite suitable icing.

This recipe was given to me by Henrietta Minner of Hartly, Delaware. It's a dish from Queen Anne county, Maryland. Her mother made White Potatoe Pie for her family quite often, because there were plently of potatoes on their farm. If mashed potatoes were left over from a dinner, she would make this pie.

WHITE POTATO PIE
Henrietta Minner

4 cups potatoes (mashed)
1 stick oleo
1 cup sugar
1 can (12 oz.) evaporated milk
3 eggs
juice from one lemon
¼ tsp. nutmeg

Mix throughly and together. Pour in a pie shell. Bake 350° untile knife comes out clean. Put salt in the potatoes when you boil them.

"Behold, how good and how pleasant it is for brethren to dwell together in unity!
Psalm133:1

137

PERFECT MERINGUE

Beat 3 egg whites (room temperature). When they bigin to foam, add ¼ tsp. cream of tartar. Now beat in ⅔ cup sugar. Sprinkle in slowly and beat well after each addition. Beat until you can not feel any sugar crystals between your fingers. When this is beaten so it stands in small peaks, fold in remaining sugar and ½ tsp. vanilla. Use mixing spoon and fold in as carefully as you would an Angel Food Cake. Pile the meringue over the thoroughly cooled pie. Bake in a 350° oven. It will start to brown in 8 minutes. It will be done in 10-12 minutes. When done, place on wire rack free from draft to cool.

Never skimp on meringue. For an attractive appearance, place in rough mounds. To cut pie, cut through the meringue only, then clean knife and cut through filling and crust.

PERFECT PIE CRUST

This recipe is enough for 2 crusts; you can either make a 2 crust pie or keep one in the refrigerator in Tupperwae or a Zip-Lock bag for future use.

2 cups flour
½ tsp. salt
⅔ cup shortening (not oil)
6 Tbsp. + 2 tsp. ice water

Sift the dry ingredients together. Cut in the shortening with a pastry blender. Toss the mixture up from the bottom of the bowl and add the ice water in very small amounts, tossing the dough up between each addition of water. Don't stir. Turn the mixture out onto waxed paper. Press the dough with the hands gently through the paper to form a round ball. Divide into 2 balls. Chill before rolling crust for 1 hour.

Rub flour into a canvas covered dough board. Use a cloth covered rolling pin. The legs from a child pantyhose works really well. Dust lightly with flour. Work from the center of dough to the edge of the chilled dough. Roll in a circle about ¼ inch thick. Fold dough to make a semi-circle. Lift the dough carefully and place in pie pan. Do not stretch! Make a hem on the dough by turning under and around the pie pan and flute the edges. Chill again. If you bake it unfilled, prick the sides and bottom of the crust with the tines of a fork. If you fill the crust, there will be no sogginess if you chill the crust for 1 hour. This sets and drys the pastry. Half fill the pastry, put in the oven and then finish filling the crust to prevent spilling. Always cool on a rack, so the air will pass under pan.

Rhubard has been overlooked too long.

RHUBARB CUSTARD PIE

3 eggs (beaten)
2⅔ cups milk
2 cups sugar
¼ cup flour
¾ tsp. numeg
3½ cups rhubarb (coarsely cut)
pastry for 1 (9") 2 crust pie
1 Tbsp. butter

Beat eggs and milk; stir in sugar, flour, nutmeg, and rhubarb. Pour into pie pan lined with crust. Dot with butter. Cover with top crust. Split for air vents in center of top crust. Bake at 400° for 15-20 minutes. Reduce to 350° until done. If browns too quickly, put a ring of aluminum foil around edge.

BLANCH HATTON'S CREAM PECAN PIE

3 eggs
1 cup evaporated milk
3 Tbsp. melted butter
½ tsp. salt
½ tsp. allspice
1 tsp. grated orange rind
1 cup pecans
1 (9") unbaked pie shell
1 cup syrup

Beat eggs slightly. Add syrup and milk. Mix well. Fold in butter, salt, allspice, and orange rind. Pour the pecans in the unbaked pie shell. Pour the custard mixture over the pecans. Bake at 350° for about 40 minutes. If the crust edge is browning too fast, place a ring of foil around the edge of the curst. Cool before serving.

This is one of today's recipes. Who can blame a young working mother who wants to give her family good and quick dessert for taking short cuts.

QUICK APPLE DUMPLINGS

2 cups Bisquit mix
soft butter or margarine
2 cups finely diced apples
cinnamon to taste
sugar
½ cup nuts or raisins

Prepare biscuit mix according to package directions. Roll out ½" thick on floured board. Spread with butter. Mix apples, cinnamon, sugar to taste and nuts. Spread over dough, roll up and cut in ¾" slices. Bring ¾ cup sugar and ½ cup water to boiling point; pour syrup into muffin tins or baking dish. Place apple rolls over syrup. Bake at 450° for 15-20 minutes.

CHEWY PECAN SQUARES

¼ cup shortening
1 cup brown sugar (packed)
1 egg
1 tsp. vanilla
¼ tsp. salt
1 cup flour
1 tsp. baking powder
⅔ cups pecans

Cream shortening and sugar together. Beat in egg, vanilla and salt thoroughly. Sift flour with baking powder and blend into mixture. Stir in nuts. Spread in 9"x9" greased pan. Bake about 30 minutes at 350°. When partially cooled, cut into squares. This recipe can be doubled or oven trippled with good results.

SWEET POTATO COBBLER
Gladys Lenox
Douglasville, Georgia

2 sweet potatoes (baking size)
1½ cups sugar
1 Tbsp. flour
½ tsp. salt
¼ grated whole nutmeg
1 cup water
1 stick butter
pastry

142

Peel potatoes and cut in thin slices. Place in deep casserole dish. Combine sugar, flour, salt, and nutmeg. Add to potatoes along with cup of water. Cut butter in pieces and lay over ingredients. Cover with pastry. Bake at 350° for 45 minutes or until brown. Serves 6.

EASY APPLE COBBLER

2½ cups canned sliced pie
    apples
1½ cups sugar
1 cup orange juice
3 Tbsp. butter,
¾ cup flour
½ tsp. salt
1 tsp. baking powder
½ cup milk

Combine apples, sugar, orange juice, and butter in saucepan; bring to a boil. Combine remaining sugar, flour, salt, and baking powder. Stir in milk and remaining melted butter separately. Pour butter into greased baking dish, add apple mixture. Bake at 350°-400°. When cobbler is done, the batter will rise to top of dish and be brown.

BERRY COBBLER

1 (#2) can of berries (any fruit may be used)
2 cups water
1 Tbsp. cornstarch

Place the above ingedients in a deep baking dish. Cover with a rich biscuit dough made with

2 cups flour (sifted, all purpose)
¼ cup sugar
½ cup fat
2½ tsp. baking powder
1 scant cup sweet milk
½ tsp. salt

Mix the crust like baking powder biscuits. Roll crust really thin. Measure to more than cover the size of baking dish. Pour the fruit in pan. If any scraps are left, put in fruit in small pieces. Then put the crust on top. Close top by pressing to the dish. Sprinkle with sugar and dot with butter. Cook at 425° for 10 minutes; then reduce to 350°. Bake until crust is brown. Prick for air vent near center. This is the way all cobblers were made in the olden days.

MRS. MILLS'
SOUR CREAM APPLE PIE

Combine
½ cup granulated sugar

with
½ Tbsp. flour
½ tsp. salt
¼ tsp. cinnamon
¼ tsp. nutmeg
1 cup sour dairy cream
¼ cup brown sugar

toss with
6 peeled cored, sliced
      tart apples

Arrange in 8" unbaked pie shell. Cover loosely with foil. Bake in hot oven at 400° for 50-55 minutes or until apples are tender. Remove foil, combine 1 cup sour dairy cream and ¼ cup brown sugar. Pour evenly over apples. Sprinkle with nutmeg. Bake 3 or 4 minutes longer.

Good to cook when you don't want to heat the oven.

STOVE-TOP RICE PUDDING

1 cup long grain rice
(uncooked)
2 cups water
½ tsp. salt
5 eggs
½ cup sugar
½ cup raisins
3 Tbsp. butter
1 tsp. vanilla
1 qt. cream (milk, or part
    evaporated milk)

Bring to boil; rice, water and salt. Stir and cover, cut burner and simmer. Cool 6-7 minutes. Add 1 quart milk. Turn to lowest setting. Cook slowly 30-40 minutes. Mix beaten eggs, sugar and raisins. Add slowly to rice mixture. Cook 1-2 minutes. Pour into custard cups. Serve hot or cold. Sugar and cinnamon may be sprinkled on top.

MY MOTHER'S OLD-FASHIONED BANANA PUDDING

⅓ cup cornstarch
½ tsp. salt
¾ cup sugar
4 cups milk
¼ cup butter
1 tsp. vanilla
3 dozen vanilla wafers
4-5 sliced bananas

Combine first 3 ingredients with 1 cup milk. Scald remaining milk; add cornstarch mixture. Stir over medium heat until thickened. Reduce heat; add butter and vanilla. Cool. Alternate layers of vanilla wafers, bananas and pudding in a large shallow dish and chill. May be topped with whip cream.

HOT FUDGE PUDDING
a really good dessert

1 cup flour
2 tsp. baking powder
¼ tsp. salt
¼ cup sugar
2 Tbsp. cocoa
½ cup milk
2 Tbsp. melted shortening
1 cup chopped nuts
1 cup brown sugar (packed)

Sift together first 5 ingredients. Stir in milk and shortening. Mix until smooth; add nuts. Spread mixture into square baking pan. Sprinkle with brown sugar mixed with 4 Tbsp. of cocoa. Pour 1¾ cup hot water evenly over batter. Bake for 350° for 40-50 minutes. Cool and cut into squares. Serve topped with any of the remaining sauce.

This is a really old recipe. It was served to our graduating class for our Senior Dinner of 1932. I don't remember anything else we had for dinner, but I remember this dessert very well. We were not used to anything that fancy during the Depression Days.

HEAVENLY HASH

1 (#2) can pineapple chunks
20 large marshmallows
¼ cup maraschino cherries
    (quartered)
1 cup heavy cream (whipped)
½ cup pecans (chopped in
    small pieces)
shredded coconut

Drain pineapple, reserve ¼ cup of syrup. Combine pineapple, reserved syrup, marshmallows, and cherries. Mix lightly. Let stand for 1 hour. Fold in whipped cream; spoon into dessert dishes. Chill. Sprinkle with nuts and coconuts.

Before the days of miniature marshmallows, large marshmallows had to be cut up with kitchen scissors dipped in glass of water.

DARK CHESS PIE

1 cup sugar
3 Tbsp. cornmeal
3 Tbsp. cocoa
3 eggs (well-beaten)
½ cup butter (melted)
½ cup light corn syrup
1 tsp. vanilla
1 (9") unbaked pie shell

Mix sugar, cornmeal and cocoa. Combine eggs, margarine, corn syrup, and vanilla. Add to sugar mixture. Stir unti smooth. Pour into pie shell (unbaked). Bake 10 minutes in 450° oven. Reduce heat to 325° for 35 minutes, or until pie tests done. You can remove from oven, if it has a circle the size of a silver dollar that's not set. It will finish as it cools. If the crust browns too fast, put a collar of aluminum foil around the edge of crust.

"Our help is in the name of the Lord, who made heaven and earth."
Psalm124:8

If you like lemon, you can't beat this.

LEMON CHESS PIE

2 cups sugar
1 Tbsp. meal
2 Tbsp. flour
4 eggs (beaten)
¼ cup milk
¼ cup lemon juice
½ cup butter (melted)
3 Tbsp. grated lemon rind
1 (9") unbaked pie shell

Combine sugar, cornmeal, flour, and cornstarch. Stir in eggs. Add milk, lemon juice, butter, and lemon rind; mix well. Bake 450° for 10 minutes. Reduce heat to 325° for 30 minutes longer or until custard test done.

"Let your light so shine before men, that they may see your good works, and glorify your Father which is in heaven."
Matthew 5:16

LOIS ALLEN'S FRIED PIES

2 cups flour
¼ tsp. salt
1 stick oleo
1 egg yolk
⅓ cup hot milk

Mix flour, salt and oleo together until mixture is like course cornmeal. Beat egg yolk, add hot milk, pour into flour mixture. Mix well; dough will be soft and smooth. Divide dough into about 10 balls, roll on floured board. Put fruit pie filling on 1 side, wet edges with water, fold over and press with fork to seal. Pierce each pie fork several times. Fry in hot oil until golden brown on both sides.

MEXICAN APPLE PIE

Patsy Hunt
Nashville, Tennessee

8-10 tortillas
4 cups apples
2 tsp. cinnamon
1 stick margarine
2 cups water
1½ cups sugar

Melt margarine in 9"x13" pan. Peel and slice apples. Sprinkle apples with cinnamon, mixed with ½ cup of the sugar. Place ½ cup of apples in 1 tortilla and roll up. Place with seam down in melted margarine. Dissolve sugar into the boiling water. Put tortillas in pan. Pour sugar and water mixture over tortillas. Cook and cover with foil for 30 minutes at 350° and cook for another 30 minutes.

COOKIES

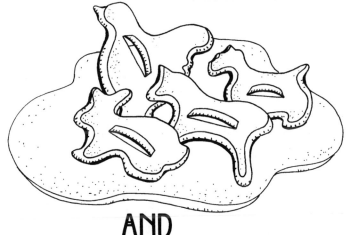

AND

CANDIES

HOW TO CHURN BUTTER

Churning was about the most monotonous thing we had to do. After you put the separated milk (sour) and the sour cream in the 3 gallon crock churn, we wrapped a cuptowel around the dasher to keep from spattering on the floor. Of course, we could sit down. We usually studied our lessons, and sometimes we sang "Here, we go around the Mulberry Bush, the Mulberry Bush, the Mulberry Bush (repeat and end with 'My Fair Lady')."

The churn had a dasher and a crock lid with a hole in the center for the dasher to go through. We filled the churn over half full. The dasher had 2 slats (made of wood) making a cross on one end of the stick like a broom handle. The stick is about 18" above the lid, and the dasher sets on the bottom of the churn. The dasher goes up and down, up and down. As it goes up and down, the motion agitates the cream thus producing butter in about 20-30 minutes if you are lucky. The temperature of the cream controls the time it take to make butter. A little hot water poured in the churn mixed with the dasher will help gather the butter. If the water was too hot, the butter will be inferior, soft and puffy, but it will take less time to make. If the cream was too cold, it would make little balls and wouldn't stick together. It didn't take a rocket scientist to learn when to put in the hot water. You learned it pretty young. Marie and I would take turns churning.

The butter then could be molded if it was cold weather. It was only molded, if it was to be sold. Our butter was put in a big bowl in the middle of the table. The hot biscuits were passed first, and we opened them with a table knife which made the knife hot. So while the butter was being passed, each one was fanning the knife in the air to cool it off so we could slice the butter. If we didn't, the butter would really slide off the knife. Those hot biscuits were so good with sorghum molasses. The first butter molds were round and had a design in the lid. Latter, they came in rectangular shapes to stack better.

154

THE SEPARATOR

After the milking was done, it had to be separatored with Deleval separator on the back porch. I never did understand how it worked, but it did. The discs had to be washed each time, as well as, the tank and spouts. The cream came out of one spout and the skimmed milk came from the other. Some of the whole milk was put in a big mixing bowl or a granite dishpan. Cream would rise better in the flatter pans rather than the round crocks. This is what we churned to make that good buttermilk. We could churn just cream, made good butter, but no buttermilk to make those good buttermilk biscuits, pound cakes, pies, for drinking, and all the other good things we had on the farm.

If a hole came in those enamel saucepans, stewers as they were called them, we just repaired them with a "Mend It" - a package with several sizes of rivets, washers and brads. You would choose the one that would cover the hole properly. It was good as new and would increase the life of the pan at a fraction of the cost of a pan.

Mrs. Hodges is 102 years old and lives in a nursing home. She still signs her own checks with a beautifully written signature. I've used this recipe for over 20 years.

PEANUT BUTTER COOKIES
Mrs. Frank Hodges

Cream together
½ granulated sugar
½ cup brown sugar
½ cup shortening
½ cup peanut butter

add
1 beaten egg

add and mix
1 tsp. soda
½ tsp. salt
½ tsp. vanilla

to
1½ cups flour

add to creamed mixture and chill. Roll in walnut size balls. Place on cookie sheet and press with fork. Bake in 350° oven about 10 minutes.

SNICKERDOODLES
Cindy Caughran
my husband's niece

1 cup shortening
1½ cups sugar
2 eggs
2¾ cups sifted flour
2 tsp. cream of tartar
1 tsp. baking soda
½ tsp. salt

Mix together really well, shortening, sugar and eggs. Sift together and then stir in flour, cream of tartar, soda and salt. Chill dough. Roll in balls walnut size. Roll mixutre of 2 Tbsp. sugar and 1 tsp. cinnamon. Place about 2 inches apart on a ungreased baking sheet. Bake 400° oven for 8-10 minutes or until lightly brown, but still soft. These cookies will puff up at first and then flatten out with crumbled tops.

CHOCOLATE CHEESE DROP COOKIES
yields 6 dozen

1½ cup sugar
½ cup butter
½ cup shortening
1 (3 oz.) pkg. cream cheese
1 egg beaten
2 Tbsp. milk
1 tsp. vanilla
½ tsp. salt
2 (1 oz.) squares of chocolate
        (unsweetened)
2¼ cup flour
1½ tsp. baking powder
½ cup finely chopped walnuts
walnut halves

Cream the first 4 ingredients. Mix in egg, milk, vanilla and salt. Melt chocolate over hot water; stir into batter. Stir in chopped nuts. Drop from tsp. onto greased baking sheet. Put walnut half on each cookie. Bake 350° for 12 minutes. Don't over cook.

MARIE MILLS' OATMEAL COOKIES

Mix in order given:

2 cups granulated sugar
1 box brown sugar
1 lb. margarine
4 eggs (beaten)
1 small box (25 ¢) oatmeal (5
     cups, quick-cooking)
3 cups + scant ⅓ cup flour with salt
1 large package of choclate chips
1½ Tbsp. salt
1½ Tbsp. soda

Add salt and baking soda to the flour. Add last 1 small box of quick-cooking oats and 1 large package of chocolate chips. This recipe makes a lot. You can freeze in rolls, slice and cook when needed. Bake at 350° for 10-12 minutes.

DATE COOKIES

2 cups brown sugar
2 eggs (well-beaten)
1 cup shortening
3½ cups flour
1 tsp. vanilla
1 cup nuts (chopped)
1 cup dates (chopped)
2 Tbsp. sweet milk
1 tsp. cream of tartar
1 tsp. soda
a few drops of maple flavor

Sift flour, mesure, and sift with baking soda and cream of tartar. Cream shortening and sugar. Add eggs and milk. Add dry ingredients, dates, nuts, and flavorings. Mix thoroughly. Form into a loaf. Chill overnight. Slice thin. Place on a well-oiled cookie sheet. Bake in a hot oven at 410° for 10 minutes.

BLACK WALNUT COOKIES

1 cup butter
1 egg
¼ tsp. nutmeg
1 cup brown sugar
3 cups flour
¼ tsp. salt
1 tsp. vanilla
1 tsp. black walnut flavor

Cream butter and sugar. Add egg and beat well. Sift flour, measure, and sift with salt and nutmeg. Add to creamed mixture. Add flavorings, mix thoroughly. Form into rolls about 1" in diameter. Cut in thin slices. Place on slightly oiled baking sheet. Bake in hot oven 410° for about 10 minutes.

THE BEST EVER SUGAR COOKIE

1 cup powdered sugar
1 cup grandulated sugar
1 cup butter
1 cup vegetable oil
2 eggs
4 cups + 4 heaping Tbsp. flour
1 tsp. salt
1 tsp. baking soda
1 tsp. cream of tartar
1 tsp. vanilla
1 tsp. almond extract

Cream together the 2 sugars, butter and oil until light and fluffy. Beat in the eggs and add the following: flour, salt, soda, cream of tartar, and extracts. Mix well. Chill dough about an hour. Roll in small balls and place on cookie sheet. Flatten with glass dipped in sugar. Bake at 350° about 10 minutes.

I've used this recipe for over 40 years.

BUTTERSCOTCH COOKIES
Kathryne Woodward

1 cup butter
2 cups brown sugar (packed)
2 eggs
3 cups flour (sifted)
1 tsp. soda

1 tsp. cream of tartar
1 cup chopped nuts

Cream first 3 ingredients well, add soda, cream of tartar to flour. Mix gradually to the creamed mixture. Add nuts. Chill in rolls. Freeze, if necessary. Slice and bake in 400° oven for 10-12 minutes. Don't over cook.

NO BAKE COOKIES

Combine and bring to a boil
2 cups sugar
¼ cup cocoa
½ cup milk
¼ lb. margarine

Remove from fire and add immediately
3 cups oatmeal (uncooked)
1 tsp. vanilla
pinch of salt
½ cup peanut butter

and if desired, add
½ cup nuts
½ cup coconut

Mix well quickly and drop from spoon on wax paper. Let set ½ hour before serving

TEXAS RANGER COOKIES

Cream together
1 cup butter or margarine
1 cup granulated sugar
1 cup brown sugar (packed)

add
2 eggs
2 cups corn flakes
2 cups quick cooking oats
1 cup flour
1 tsp. baking powder
1 tsp. vanilla
1 cup coconut
1 cup nuts (optional)

Mix and drop from spoon on a greased cookie sheet. Bake 12-15 minutes at 325°. Do not overcook.

CHOCOLATE COOKIES

2 cups sugar
½ cup cocoa
½ cup butter
½ cup milk Pinch of salt
1 tsp. vanilla
2 cups rolled oats (quick cook-
      ing oats work well)

Combine first 4 ingredients in sauce pan. Bring to a boil. Cook 2½ minutes. Stir constantly. Remove from heat, immediately. Quickly add remaining ingredients. Stir until oats are well-coated. If desired, you could add coconut, nuts and raisins. Drop onto wax paper. Let stand about ½ hour. Store as usual. Especially good with milk.

I would say store in a cookie jar. We didn't have one; didn't need one. We didn't have a lot of snacks, so they were gone quickly unless my mother hid some for our dinner. To keep our school dinner bucket from rusting, there were nail holes punched in the lid.

BUTTERSCOTCH PECAN COOKIES
a crispy cookie

1 stick oleo
1½ cups brown sugar
    (packed)
2-2½ cups flour
1 tsp. vanilla
1 egg
1 cup pecans

Cream butter, sugar. Add vanilla. Add egg and blend well. Add flour and nuts and mix until all flour is moistened. Drop by tsp. on to a baking sheet. Bake in 350° oven for about 12 minutes. Do not overcook.

I was told by Lou Kerr that Aunt Bill who originated this candy was related to the Kerr's. Robert Kerr was a very powerful U. S. senator from Oklahoma. It was said he could have moved the Lincoln Memorial to Oklahoma if he so desired.

AUNT BILL'S BROWN CANDY

3 pints white sugar
¼ lb. margarine
1 tsp. vanilla
1 pint milk or cream
¼ tsp. salt
1 lb. pecans (broken)

Pour 1 pint sugar in heavy skillet and place over a low fire. Stir constantly to prevent scorching. Pour remaining 2 pints sugar and the milk or cream in a deep heavy kettle. Put over low heat to cook slowly while the sugar is melting in the skillet. As soon as all the sugar is melted, begin pouring it into the kettle of boiling cream and sugar, keeping it on very low heat and stirring constantly. Pour a very fine stream no larger than a knitting needle and stir across the bottom of the kettle all the time. Continue cooking and stirring until the mixture forms a firm ball in cold water. Turn out fire and add soda, quickly stirring vigorously as it foams up. Add margarine, allowing it to melt as you stir. Set off the fire for about 10 minutes.

Add vanilla and start beating with a wooden spoon. Beat until the mixture is thick and heavy, having a dull appearance. Add nuts and mix, and roll out onto wax paper and shape into 2 small rolls or one large one. Keep wrapped in wax paper and slice off candy as needed. Keeps indefinitely and stays moist and fresh, as long as you keep it wrapped in wax paper.

PECAN ROLL

2 cups sugar
½ cup corn syrup
1 cup cream
1 cup light brown sugar
1½ cups pecans

Boil cream, sugar and syrup to soft ball stage (234° - 238°). Cool to room temperature. Beat until creamy. Turn onto board dusted with powdered sugar. Knead until firm. Shape into a roll and cover outside with pecan meats. Put in cool place to harden. Slice when firm, using a sharp knife. Finely chopped pecan meats may be worked through the candy while it is being kneaded, if desired.

NOVA CROW'S
BUTTERMILK FUDGE

1 tsp. soda
1 cup buttermilk
2 cups sugar
2 Tbsp. corn syrup
1 stick margarine
1 cup nuts

Blend soda and buttermilk, stirring well. Pour sugar in large saucepan; add buttermilk mixture, corn syrup and margarine. Bring to a boil; cook to 240° on a candy thermometer or medium soft ball stage. Remove from heat and beat well. Stir in nuts. Drop by spoonfuls on wax paper or pour in candy dish.

Pralines came from Europe. The original recipe used the hard to find walnuts. A new flavor was created with the pecans.

PRALINES

3 cups sugar
1 cup heavy cream
3 Tbsp. butter
a dash of salt
3 cups pecan pieces
2 tsp. vanilla

Caramelize 1 cup sugar. Place remaining sugar, cream, butter, and salt in a heavy saucepan. Cook until blended. Add caramelize sugar and cook to soft ball stage. Cool naturally to room temperature. Add vanilla and pecans. Beat until creamy. Drop from teaspoon onto wax paper.

OH! SO GOOD FUDGE

2 cups sugar
1 small can evaporated milk
12 large marshmallows
2 Tbsp. water
½ cup nut meats
¼ lb. butter or margarine
¼ cup chocolate chips
2 tsp. vanilla

Bring sugar and milk to boil in heavy saucepan. Boil 8 minutes. Melt marshmallows in water in top of double boiler. In large bowl, put butter, chocolate chips, nuts, and vanilla. Add the hot sugar, milk mixture and melted marshmallows. Let cool and beat until it is thick enough to hold its form. Put in an 8"x8" pan. Place in refrigerator until firm enough to cut into squares. It will not harden for several hours. Easy, fool-proof and melts in your mouth!

"But seek ye first the kingdom of God, and his righteousness; and all these things shall be added unto you.
Matthew 6:33

167

EASY KARO CANDY

1⅓ cup margarine
½ cup white Karo syrup
1 lb. powdered sugar (sifted)
1 tsp. vanilla

Stir margarine, Karo syrup and half of the sugar over low heat until bubbly. Quickly stir in rest of the sugar and vanilla. Remove from heat. Beat until mixture just holds shape. Knead quickly until smooth. Cool to luke warm. Put in a greased pan. Slice when firm.

PEANUT PATTIES
so good and creamy

2 cups sugar
¾ tsp. soda
2 cups raw peanuts or
(pecans) 1 cup half & half
or
½ cup evaporated milk and ½
    cup whole milk

Combine sugar and soda. Stir in gradually the milk. Bring to boil over medium heat, stirring occasionally. Reduce heat, cook, stirring occasionally to soft ball stage or 324° on candy thermometer. Remove from heat; add butter immediately. Add nuts. Beat mixture for 3 minutes or until smooth. Drop from metal spoon on wax paper. Add small amount of hot water, if necessary. Yields 24-30 patties.

POPCORN CRUMBLE

2 quarts unsalted popped corn
1½ cups pecan halves
⅔ cups almonds (sliced)
1⅓ cups sugar
1 cup margarine
½ cup white corn syrup
2 tsp. vanilla

Mix popcorn and nuts into a large bowl, set aside. Combine sugar, syrup and margarine. Bring to a quick boil; stir constantly and cook to 300° using a candy thermometer. Add vanilla and very quickly pour over popcorn and nut mixture. Stir to coat well and spread on a greased cookie sheet to harden. When mixture has harden, break into serving size pieces.

"A good tree cannot bring forth evil fruit, neither can a corrupt tree bring forth good fruit."
Matthew 7:18

POPCORN BALLS
Olevia Robinson

½ lb. popcorn
⅔ cup corn syrup
2 cups sugar
⅔ cup boiling water
2 tsp. cream of tartar
2 Tbsp. vinegar
2 Tbsp. melted butter
2 tsp. vanilla flavoring
⅛ tsp. soda

Pop corn. Place in large pan. Combine syrup, sugar, water, and vinegar. Heat to boiling. Add cream of tartar. Boil to soft crack stage (275° - 280°). Remove from fire. Add butter, baking soda and flavoring. Pour over popcorn. Form into balls.

Mike Allen and Sylvia Allen Worcester

This old photo of Thelma's son and daughter is the inspiration for this book's cover photo.

BREADS

Breads come in 2 categories - quick and slow. The quick breads use baking powder; the slow ones use yeast.

THE ELECTROLUX GAS REFRIGERATOR

The Electrolux was an early brand of gas refrigerator used in the late '30s and early '40s. They weren't as efficient as those manufactured now, but they were a wonderful improvement and very effective cost wise. I don't know why they quit making them. Our rates were much lower then. Fifty cents a month would cover the cost of operation. This was when everybody began making icebox rolls. My mother-in-law, Lou Allen, made them. She would take them out of the Electrolux on Sunday before going to Sunday school, and they were ready to cook when she got home from church. This is her recipe that's over 50 years old.

LOU ALLEN'S ELECTROLUX ROLLS

1 yeast cake
⅓ cup sugar
1½ tsp. salt
2 cups luke warm water
3 Tbsp. shortening
2 cups whole wheat flour
4½ cups regular flour

Break yeast into bowl; add sugar, salt and water. Add melted shortening. Make sure it isn't hot, because the heat will kill the yeast. I use liquid shortening now; it wasn't available back then. Add the whole wheat flour and melted shortening to make a soft dough. Add the remaining regular flour to make a stiff dough. Place on a dough board and knead. There will be enough flour left to knead with. You 'll want to knead about 10 minutes. That's important. Place in a mixing bowl with 1 Tbsp. of melted shortening, turn with the greased side up. Cover and let rise in a draft free place for 2 hours. Punch down. Use flour on hands to knead, if necessary. Roll on dough board to ¾" thickness. If you want a soft roll, place close together in a baking pan; if you want a crusty roll, leave about 1" apart. Cover and put in refrigerator. It will keep for several days. Let rise for 2 hours in a warm place before baking. Bake at 350° for about 20 minutes.

MRS. ODEN'S HOMINY GRITS SPOON BREAD

2 cups milk
1 tsp. salt
1 scant cup hominy grits
1 Tbsp. butter
3 eggs (separated)
1 tsp. baking powder

Scald milk and add salt and grits. Cook until thickens. Add the butter and set aside until slightly cool. Add the well-beaten egg yolks. Beat egg whites stiff, gradually adding baking powder. Fold egg whites in hominy grits. Bake at 350° for about 40 minutes in a well-greased baking dish. Dip out with a spoon to serve.

Mrs. Mills was such a wonderful cook and taught me so much.

MRS. MILLS'
BUTTERMILK BISCUITS

2 cups sifted flour (level cups)
2½ tsp. baking powder
¼ tsp. soda
½ tsp. salt
4 Tbsp. shortening
⅔ cup buttermilk (approximately)

Sift the flour. Measure. Level with a knife. Mix the baking powder, salt and soda with the flour. Cut the shortening into the flour with a pastry blender until it is like a coarse meal with no lump larger than a pea. Add the milk and stir quickly until the mixture forms a ball. It should follow a fork and not stick to the sides of the bowl. This should be done quickly not taking more than 2 minutes.

Turn the dough out on a lightly floured bowl. Knead gently for about 30 seconds to knit the dough together. Pat onto a sheet about ½" in thickness. Cut with a floured cutter. Press straight down with the cutter; do not twist the cutter. Put on slightly greased baking sheet. Biscuits need to cook in a hot oven at 450° for about 12 minutes.

When measuring the milk, use a half cup and put part of the milk in the ½ cup to be used in reserve. To see if needed, form the ball that won't stick to side of the bowl. If you like biscuits with a crust, place them where they do not touch each other. If you like less crust, they can touch. Mrs. Mills would say, "For goodness sake, don't cut them with a knife. Always break biscuits open." If your biscuits aren't perfect, then you didn't follow directions carefully. Best served hot!

The only one I've ever known who could make crackers.

LOU ALLEN'S SODA CRACKERS

4 cups flour
2 Tbsp. sugar
1 tsp. salt
¼ cup butter
1 cup milk

Sift together flour, salt and sugar. Cut in butter until mealy. Stir in enough to make a stiff dough. Roll ¼" thick. Cut with a cooky cutter. Place on an ungreased cookie sheet. Prick the top in many places with a fork. Brush with milk gently. Bake at 450° for 15-18 minutes or until golden brown. I sprinkle tops lightly with salt before serving.

CORNBREAD
Lois Allen

1 cup cornmeal (I prefer yellow)
2 tsp. brown sugar (I use 1 tsp.)
½ tsp. baking soda
2 eggs (well-beaten)
1 cup flour
1 tsp. salt
1 tsp. baking powder
¼ cup shortening (melted)
1½ cups buttermilk

Sift flour, measure and sift with baking soda, salt and baking powder. Mix wih cornmeal. Combine shortening, sugar and eggs. Add sour milk and combine with dry ingredients. Beat only until smooth. Pour into smoking hot, well oiled pan ¾ full. Bake in at 425° oven for 25-30 minutes. Serves 8.

MARIE MILLS' DATE NUT BREAD
an old recipe

1½ cup dates
1½ cups boiling water
½ cup sugar
½ cup shortening
1 tsp. salt
1 egg
2¾ cups flour (sifted)
1 tsp. cream of tartar
1 cup walnut meats
    (chopped)
1 tsp. vanilla

Wash and stone the dates. The way they are prepared now, the first step is not necessary. Cuts dates in quarters and pour the boiling water over them. Add shortening, sugar and salt. When cool, add flour with soda, cream of tartar, nuts and vanilla. Gently combine ingredients. Pour in a greased loaf pan and bake at 350° for about 1 hour.

Betty Gilliam loves to cook and gives most of it away.

GRAPENUT BREAD
Betty Gilliam

2 cups buttermilk
1 cup grapenuts
2 cups sugar
1 stick Oleo
2 eggs
2 tsp. baking powder
1 tsp. soda
3½ cups flour
1 cup pecans
a pinch of salt

Combine buttermilk, flour and grapenuts. Let stand 1 hour. Cream sugar and Oleo. Add 2 eggs one at a time, beating after each addition. Add salt, baking powder and soda to the soaked mixture. Combine the soaked mixture to the sugar mixture. Add finely chopped nuts. Pour into 2 greased loaf pans and bake for 45 minutes to 1 hour at 350°, or until done.

Myrtle Baucum was a wonderful cook. I've used this recipe since the late '50s.

BANANA NUT BREAD
in memory of Myrtle Baucum

1 cup butter
2 cups sugar
2 tsp. vanilla
2 tsp. lemon juice
4 eggs
2 cups ripe bananas (flaked
    with brown spots)
1 tsp. salt
3½ cups flour (sifted)
2 tsp. soda
2 tsp. baking powder
1 cup sour cream
1 cup nuts (chopped)

Cream butter and sugar. Add vanilla and lemon juice. Add eggs, one at a time, beating well after each addition. Add bananas. Sift salt, flour, soda, and baking powder, add alternately with sour cream and banana mixture. Fold in nuts. Pour into 2 well-greased loaf pans. Bake in 350° oven for 50-55 minutes.

HAWAIIAN BREAD
Olevia Robinson
in memory of her mother, Effie Talley

2½ cups pineapple (crushed,
    undrained)
10 oz. coconut (flaked)
4 eggs (beaten)

1½ cups sugar
4 cups flour
add to flour
2 tsp. salt
2 tsp. soda
1 cup nuts (chopped)

Combine ingredients in order given. Bake for 1 hour at 350° in 2 greased loaf pans.

STRAWBERRY BREAD
Betty Gilliam

4½ cups flour
3 cups sugar
6 eggs
3 (10 oz.) frozen strawberries
1½ tsp. soda
1 tsp. salt
1½ cups oil

Combine flour, sugar, soda, and salt. Add strawberries, eggs and oil. Makes 3 small loaves or 2 large ones. Bake at 350° for 45 minutes or until done. Good for Christmas rememberances.

"Who so causeth the righteous to go astray in an evil way, he shall fall himself into his own pit: but the upright shall have good things in possession.
Proverbs 28:10

CRANBERRY-ORANGE BREAD

2 cups flour (sifted)
¾ cup sugar
1½ tsp. baking powder
1 tsp. salt
½ tsp. soda
2 Tbsp. oil
1 cup cranberries
½ cup walnuts
1 tsp. grated orange rind
1 egg
1 cup orange juice

Sift dry ingredients. Stir in coarsely chopped nuts and grated orange rind. Combine eggs, orange juice, and salad oil. Add to dry ingredients and stir until just moistened. Bake in a greased loaf pan at 350° for about 50 minutes.

ORANGE BREAD

1 cup of orange peel. Use only the yellow part as the white is bitter. Cut into small pieces. Put in saucepan and cover with water. Cook until tender. Add 1 cup of sugar and cook until it is a medium syrup. You should have a full cup. Let cool. Sift together 4 cups flour, 2 Tbsp. baking powder, and ¼ tsp. salt. Cream together 2 Tbsp. butter, 2 eggs, ¾ cups

sugar. Add 2 cups milk and sifted dry ingredients. Beat thoroughly. Pour into 2 well-greased loaf pans. Add cook and cooled orange peel. Beat with wooden spoon 1 more minute. Bake at 350° for 40-50 minutes. Let set until cold or better yet, wait until next day to slice. Good for sandwiches.

LEMON BREAD

½ cup shortening
1 cup sugar
2 eggs (slightly beaten)
1⅔ cups flour (sifted)
1 tsp. baking powder
½ tsp. salt
½ cup milk
½ cup nuts (finely chopped)
grated peel of 1 lemon
toppings
¼ cup sugar
2 Tbsp. lemon juice

Cream shortening with sugar, add slightly beaten eggs and blend well. Mix flour with baking powder and salt. Add the flour mixture and milk to the shortening mixture. Mix well. Stir in nuts and lemon peel. Bake in a greased 5"x9" pan in 350° oven for about 1 hour. Combine with ¼ cup sugar with lemon juice. Brush over top of loaf while hot. Remove when cool enough to handle.

MARIE MILLS' PUMPKIN BREAD

½ cup vegetable oil
2 eggs
1 cup pumpkin
1⅔ cup sifted flour
1¼ cup sugar
½ tsp. soda
½ tsp. cinnamon
½ tsp. nutmeg
¼ tsp. salt

Combine oils and eggs and pumpkin in a large bowl. Mix dry ingredients together. Beat pumpkin ingredients gradually. Pour in a well-greased and floured 9"x5"x3" loaf pan. Bake about 1 hour or until tests done.

For a Christmas bread, Marie adds ½ cup of nuts and ½ cup diced candied cherries.

I had never heard of chocolate gravy until I began showing my first cookbook in Nashville, Tennessee, when a lot of people began asking about it. Sharon Wilson of Chickasha, Oklahoma, gave me the recipe. Carla Raye from Oklahoma City gave me the same recipe and suggested that you use brown sugar for change. They both said they only use it for special occasions like birthdays and company breakfast.

CHOCOLATE GRAVY
Sharon Wilson

1 cup sugar
¼ cup cocoa
¼ cup flour
1 cup water
a dash of salt
¼ cup butter
½ tsp. vanilla

Blend sugar, flour, cocoa and stir in water in a heavy saucepan over low heat, stirring constantly until the consistency of gravy. Serve on hot biscuits.

TORNADO ALLEY

The following are excerpts from a newspaper article written by Claudine Dollar for *The Altus Times-Democrat* newspaper in 1976.

"We continue with the interview with Thelma Allen and Marie Mills who were in the business district in Blair on June 16, 1928, when a tornado destroyed that section of town, killing three people, one of whom was their mother, Mrs. George Rogers. After the storm had passed and those who had miraculously escaped injury began searching through the debris for casualties, Marie and Thelma were taken to the home of their father's sister and her husband, Mr. and Mrs. J. H. Brock. They found their relatives still in the cellar...and joined them. The girls were so upset they wouldn't leave the cellar so a Mrs. Lance and a Mrs. Boyd spent the night in the cellar with them. Thelma remembers that her father came part way down the cellar steps about an hour after they got there. He didn't say anything and no one asked him any questions. He just looked in to see that they were all right and left. The next morning...their aunt came down and told them their father wanted them. Although they had know in their own minds that their mother was dead; this was the first time they had been told.

When I asked Marie to describe the condition of her father's service station after the storm, I heard another of the unbelievable stories which are always in evidence after a tornado. She said the building was completely destroyed and the concrete floor was swept clean except for a fruit jar full of milk. It seems that Rogers had a habit of keeping a jar of milk in the pop box to drink during the day. The box was the type that the lid slides to 1 side and you put ice and water in it and put the bottles in the cold water. There was no sign of the pop box after the storm but the jar of milk was left sitting, unbroken, on the concrete floor. It is possible that Rogers set the jar down on the floor for some reason but, even so, it is a mystery how it could have been left unbroken.

Mrs. Rogers had a tapestry scarf that she kept on a dresser where her customers sat to try on the hats that she made for them. Someone found that scarf a half-mile south of town and returned it to the family."

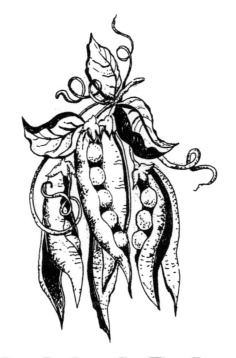

SALADS

AND

S OUPS

24 HOUR COLESLAW

1 medium head of cabbage
1 medium onion
1 medium green pepper
10 stuffed olives (optional)
½ cup sugar
½ cup salad oil
1 cup vinegar
1 tsp. salt
1 tsp. celery seed
1 tsp. dry mustard

Shred cabbage; dice onion fine. Chop green pepper; slice olives. Combine cabbage, onion, green peppers, and olives in large bowl; sprinkle with sugar. Toss to mix well. Combine salad oil, salt, vinegar, celery seed, and mustard in sauce pan, bring to boil. Boil for 3 minutes, stir occasionally. Pour over vegetable mixture; toss to mix well. Cover tightly. Refrigerate 24 hours before serving. Serves 8. It keeps for at least 6 weeks. You may want to double it.

CAULIFLOWER SALAD
(different)

2 cups diced raw cauliflower
1½ cups stuffed olives
1 medium onion (chopped fine)
6 hard cooked eggs (chopped)
3 oz. water chestnuts (sliced)

Combine all ingredients. Coat with mayonaise. Serve chilled in a bowl.

COCA COLA SALAD

1 can pie cherries
½ cup sugar
2 package cherry gelatin
½ cup pecans (chopped)
1 - 6 oz. Coca Cola (cold)
1 - No. 1 can pineapple
       (crushed)

Heat cherries, sugar and water to dissolve sugar. Add gelatin and stir until dissolved. Cool until partially set. Add nuts, pineapple and Coca Cola. Chill until firm. Yields 12 servings.

This recipe from Buelah Campbell Russon was given to me by her granddaughter Donna Williams of Murfreesboro, Tennessee. Donna says her "granny" was a wonderful lady and a good ole country cook; and when Donna left Granny's house she was always "full as a tick."

GRANNY RUSSOM'S
HOT MASHED TATER SALET

4 or 5 large 'arsh' taters
½ cup milk
1 or 2 Tbsp. Blue Plate
Mayonaise
2 or 3 hard-boiled eggs
1 tsp. mustard
1 onion (chopped)
2 or 3 sweet pickles (chopped)
salt and pepper to taste

Peel and cube potatoes. Boil until tender. Drain water and mash potatoes. Add milk, mayonaise, mustard, salt, and pepper. Mash all ingredients thoroughly. Add chopped boiled eggs, chopped onion and chopped pickle. Stir together. Serve "tater salet" with pinto beans and a pone of cornbread.

EASTER SALAD

1 package lemon gelatin
10 oz. package marshmallows
1 pint whipping cream
        (whipped)
1 - 3 oz. package cream
        cheese (softened)

188

1 cup salad dressing
1 - No. 2 can pineapple
    (crushed)
2 cups water (boiling)

Dissolve lemon gelatin in boiling water. Add marshmallows to hot gelatin to melt. Cool until partially set. Whip cream cheese with whipped cream. Add salad dressing and pineapple to cream mixture. Fold into cooled lemon mixture. Pour into molds. When firm, pour prepared cherry gelatin over first mixture. Cool. Serves 8-12.

CHERRY CRANBERRY SALAD

1 package cherry gelatin
2 cups boiling water
1 apple
1 orange
1 can whole cranberry sauce
1 cup celery (finely chopped)
½ cup nuts (chopped)

Add boiling water to gelatin. Mix until dissolved and cool until partially set. Grind apple and orange in food chopper or blender. Add apple, orange, celery, nuts, and cranberry sauce to gelatin. Mix well and cool until firm.

FOR GOODNESS SAKE SALAD

2 packages lime gelatin
2 packages lemon gelatin
1 - No. 2 can pineapple
      (crushed)
1 envelope unflavored gelatin
1 cup cottage cheese
1 cup evaporated milk
1 cup salad dressing
½ cup nuts (chopped)
½ cup maraschino cherries
      (chopped)

Dissolve lime and lemon gelatin in 2 cups hot water. Add 2 cups cold water and pineapple. Let stand until mixture starts to thicken. Add unflavored gelatin that has been mixed with ¼ cup cold water, blend well. Add remaining ingredients. Pour into 9"x12" baking dish. Chill until firm. Cut into squares. Serve topped with additional salad dressing and half maraschino cherry. Yields 18 servings.

THREE-LAYER GELATIN SALAD

1 box cherry gelatin
1 box lemon gelatin
1 box strawberry gelatin
40 miniature marshmallows
1 small pkg. cream cheese
1 - No. 2 can pineapple
    (crushed and drained)
¾ cup whipping cream
    (whipped)
1 bottle maraschino cherries
    (diced)

Mix cherry gelatin with 1 cup boiling water to dissolve. Add 1 cup cold water and pour into square pan. Mix lemon gelatin in the same manner and add cream cheese and marsh-mallows. Cool. Add pineapple and cherries and set aside to partially thicken. Add whipped cream to lemon mixture and pour over cherry gelatin which is firm. Mix strawberry gelatin. Cool and pour over lemon layer. Cool until firm and cut in squares. Yields 16 servings.

This recipe was given to Mrs. Griffis by a traveling salesman who obtained it from a woman who operated a boarding house where he stayed. It has to be old because you place the salad in the ice box to harden overnight.

MARSHMALLOW SALAD

3 eggs
juice of 3 lemons
1 lb. marshmallows
1 cup sweet milk
1 pint sweet cream (whipped)
1 lb. pecans
1 lb. grapes or white cherries
1 can pineapples (diced).

Beat eggs well. Add lemon juice to eggs and beat again. Heat sweet milk to boiling point. Add marshmallows, eggs and lemon juice. Stir until marshmallows melt; continue stirring until cool. When cool, pour in 1 pint sweet cream (whipped), 1 lb. pecans, 1 lb. grapes or white cherries, and 1 can pineapples (diced). Place in ice box overnight to harden.

COTTAGE CHEESE SALAD

1 package small lemon gelatin
1 package small lime gelatin
4 cups water (boiling)
1 cup mayonaise
2 cups cottage cheese
1 cup celery (chopped)
½ cup green pepper (diced)
2 Tbsp. onion (grated)

Dissolve gelatins in boiling water. Chill until thickened. Fold in remaining ingredients. Chill until firm. Cut in squares and serve on lettuce leaf. Serves 16. This makes a lot; you may want to divide this recipe by half.

CHEESE SALAD
Prize-winning recipe by
Olevia Robinson

2 cups pineapple (crushed)
1 small pkg. lemon flavored
    Jell-O
1 Tbsp. unflavored gelatin
    (softened in 2 Tbsp. cold
    water)
juice of 1 lemon
¼ cup pimento (chopped)
½ cup nuts (chopped)
1 cup celery (chopped)
6 marshmallows (chopped in
    small pieces, I use ¾ cups
    miniature marshmallows)
1 cup whipping cream
2 - 3 oz. package cream cheese

Drain juice from pineapple and add water to make 2 cups. Heat to boiling. Pour over lemon flavored Jell-O (small package) and unflavored gelatin which has been softened in cold water. Stir until dissolved. Mix thoroughly. Cool until partially set. Add pineapple which has been mixed with cream cheese, pimento, nuts, and celery. Add marshmallows. Fold in whipped cream. Put in oblong Pyrex dish. When chilled, cut into squares or put into a mold that has been rinsed in cold water. Serves 10.

This is a great dressing; it's delicious, easy and economical to make.

MRS. MILLS' SALAD DRESSING
(mayonnaise type)

¾ cup oil
1 Tbsp. sugar
1 tsp. dry mustard
1 tsp. salt
⅛ tsp. cayenne pepper
2 egg yolks
¼ cup vinegar
3 Tbsp. cornstarch

Pour oil in mixing bowl. Mix and sift sugar, mustard, salt and cayenne pepper. This is important because dry mustard is lumpy and hard to mix with other ingredients. Add sifted seasoning to oil. Also add the egg yolks and vinegar, but do not stir. Add ½ cup of cold water to cornstarch and stir until smooth. Now add another ½ cup cold water and cook over low heat, stirring constantly until boiling point is reached and mixture becomes clear. Continue stirring for about 3 minutes. Pour cornstarch mixture on top of ingredients in mixing bowl and beat briskly with rotary beater until smooth and creamy. Chill before serving. This salad dressing should be the same thickness as regular mayonnaise and in appearance. Try on potato salad, meat, fish salads, and cold asparagus. Next time you serve avacados drop a tablespoon into each half.

RASPBERRY-LEMON VINEGAR

3 cups fresh or frozen raspberries
1 lemon
4 cups white vinegar (5% acidity)
½ cup sugar

Rinse raspberries and let air dry on a paper towel or better still a cloth towel. Place berries in a 6 quart jar. With a vegetable peeler, remove rind of lemon in a long single strip; add to jar of berries. Set aside. Combine vinegar and sugar in a saucepan; bring almost to a boil over low heat, stirring constantly, until sugar melts. Pour hot vinegar over berries. Cover jar tightly. Let stand at room temperature for 2 to 7 days. Remove lemon rind, strain vinegar through several layers of cheesecloth to remove berries. Discard berries. Store vinegar in bottles with airtight lids. Store in a cool dark place up to 6 months. Serve vinegar mixture over salad greens.

This soup is based on the dry pea. It is available the year around and nearly everywhere in the world. It is typical American. It is very nutrious and could be served as a one-dish supper without apology. It's a very thrifty dish.

SPLIT PEA SOUP

3 cups dried green split peas
1 ham bone with meat on it
3 quarts boiling water
2 large carrots (cut in chunks)
1 large onion
6 sprigs of parsley
several celery leaves
1 bay leaf
black pepper
salt

Modern packaging has eliminated the process of soaking and picking over for rocks. Soaking does shorten the cooking time. Put the peas and ham bone in a big kettle. Add the boiling water, carrots, onions, celery, and the herbs and leaves tied in a small bouquet. Bring to a boil and simmer 3-4 hours. Remove the ham bone, herbs, carrots, and onions and cool the soup. Refrigerate overnight and remove fat from surface of soup. If you want an elegant soup, pour it in a blender, add some rich cream and serve in a soup cup. For a hearty soup, leave as is. Take ham off bone and supplement it with Polish sausage or weiners. Serve with buttered cornbread.

This recipe is a quick dish that you can usually prepare if you've been shut-in for a week from a long snow storm. You can substitute dry milk for whole milk. You can also use dehydrated parsley and onion flakes in the spice rack.

OLD TIMEY POTATO SOUP

6-8 potatoes (peeled and sliced)
3 medium onions (sliced)
1½ tsp. salt
6 cups milk (scalded)
2 Tbsp. parsley (chopped)
1 cup celery (chopped)
black pepper
2 Tbsp. butter

Put the potatoes, onions and salt in a pot large enough to cover with cold water. Cook and cover; boil gently for 20 minutes. You can leave the vegetables sliced or put them in the blender or mash them to a pulp in the pan they were cooked in. Add the milk and seasoning to taste. Use plently of pepper and butter. Serve with crackers or hot cornbread.

"He tht is of a proud heart stirreth up strife: but he that putteth his trust in the Lord shall be made fat."
Proverbs 28:25

This recipe is like potato soup and can be made even if you haven't been to the market lately.

MISSION CORN CHOWDER
Juarine Wooldridge
Cassville, Missouri

½ cup salt pork (diced)
1 large onion (diced)
1 quart boiling water
3 cups whole kernel corn
    (cooked fresh or canned)
5 medium sized potatoes
(peeled and cubed)
1½ tsp. salt
1 quart milk
black pepper

Cook the diced salt pork over moderate heat. Stir occasionally to keep from becoming too brown. Remove from pan with a slotted spoon. Saute' the onion in the pork fat until just clear. Add the water, corn, potatoes, and salt, cook until the potatoes are nearly done. Add the milk and simmer for 10-15 minutes. Season to taste. I like lots of pepper. Sprinkle with salt pork. Good with soda crackers or cornbread.

This recipe was printed in an old gas company brochure.

CRAB CHOWDER

2 Tbsp. margarine
1 cup celery (diced)
1 medium onion (chopped)
2 Tbsp. flour
¼ tsp. thyme
¼ tsp. white pepper
5 cups skim milk
3 large potatoes
6 slices of cooked bacon
     (crumbled)
1 (8 oz.) can crab (flaked)

Melt margarine in large saucepan over medium heat. Stir in celery and onion; cook until tender. Blend in flour, thyme and pepper; gradually add milk, stirring constantly. Add potatoes and simmer until tender. Stir in crab and heat thoroughly. Serve with crumbled bacon.

"He that hath no rule over his own spirit is like a city that is broken down, and without walls."
Proverbs 25:28

BUSY DAY STEW
(cook in oven or crock pot)

2 lbs. beef (chuck or round) or
stew meat
8 carrots (sliced)
4 potatoes (peeled and
chopped)
3 medium onions (chopped)
1 Tbsp. salt
1 Tbsp. pepper
1 Tbsp. sugar
3 Tbsp. minute tapioca (you
could use a little rice, instant
potatoes or cornstarch)

Place all ingredients in a large covered pan. Do not brown beef first.
Bake at 250° for 5 hours. Serve with
crisp crackers or buttered hot cornbread.

FOLK MEDICINE

Our father probably had the doctor more than was necessary. He might not have paid the doctor until the cotton crop was out, but he got paid.

We used lots of home remedies, such as:

If a red ant stung you, the bite was painted with blueing; a liquid used in the laundry to keep clothes white.

For chigger bites, we rubbed them with salty meat grease. The chiggers would bury themselves in the flesh, and the salt would kill them.

If you stepped on a rusty nail or thorn, you soaked the foot in kerosene.

For a boil, we made a poultice from a scrapped potato.

For pneumonia, a mustard plaster was used on the chest. Made from dry mustard and mixed with very hot water.

During World War II, before penicillin, we rubbed camphorated oil on the chest and covered it with a hot flannel cloth. One time my aunt came to see us from some distance away, and one of her boys had burned the top of his foot with hot water - a very wicked sore. My grandmother had us gather some mussle shells from the creek bed. She dried them in the oven, mashed them into a powder and dusted it on the burn. It was well in "nothing flat." People died from blood poisoning; never heard of now. Of course, there were quinine, salts and castor oil, but my folks didn't put much faith in them. So we were spared from that awful tasting medicine.

RELISHES
AND
PRESERVES

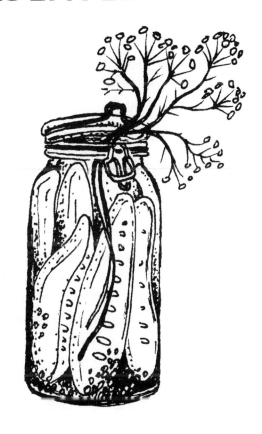

MRS. MILLS'
WATERMELLON RIND PICKLES
over 50 years old

watermellon rind
salt for brine (not iodized)
2 cups cider vinegar
7 cups sugar
2-3 cinnamon sticks
1 Tbsp. whole cloves

Select a mellon with a thick firm rind, not overripe. Trim off the peel and all of the pink meat. Cut the rind into squares. The rind will shrink, so don't cut the rind too small. Make a weak brine by adding 2 Tbsp. of salt to a gallon of cold water and put the pieces in to soak for 12 hours. At the end of this time, drain off the brine and rinse the pieces well in cold water. Then let stand in ice water (covered) for 1 hour. Drain, then cover again with water and simmer, but do not boil, until they are tender enough to prick with a toothpick. In the meantime, make a syrup by cooking the sugar with the vinegar. Add a spice bag made by tying cinnamon sticks and cloves into a cheesesbag. When the syrup has boiled for 15-20 minutes, add the squares of drained mellow rind and cook them gentley until they are set in syrup for 24 hours. Pack the rinds into sterilized jars and set in a pan of hot water. Reheat the syrup to a good boil and pour over the rind to fill the jars to the neck. Seal while hot. Believe me, these pickles are worth the effort.

CRYSTAL PICKLES

Cut large sour pickles in very thin slices. Weigh. Place in a large bowl or jar. Add an equal weight of sugar. Let stand 3 days. The pickles will become crisp and clear. A big savings, when you look at the price of sweet pickles.

"He that trusteth in his riches shall fall: but the righteous shall flourish as a branch.
Proverbs 11:28

SOUR PICKLES

3 quarts cucumbers
9 quarts water
1 cup salt (not iodized)
1½ tsp. each: whole cloves and
        allspice
2 cinnamon sticks
1 blade mace
1 small red pepper
2 quarts vinegar
2 cups sugar

Put the washed cucumbers in a crock or a stone jar. Cover them with a boiling hot brine made from the salt and water. Let stand overnight in the brine. In the morning, rinse and drain them twice. If pure vinegar is used, dilute ⅓ to ½ with water. Tie the spices in a cheesecloth bag and drop in a large kettle with the vinegar and simmer for 30 minutes. Let it come to a brisk boil for just 1 minute. Remove and place them in a crock or stone jar. When all the cucumbers have been scalded this way and placed in the crock, bring the vinegar remaining in the kettle to a boil and pour it over the cucumbers. Cover the crock closely and store the pickles for 3 weeks. In the old days we used clean old bed sheets to wrap around the crock. They were then put in the cellar where they would keep all winter. Now you would place into sterilized jars and cover them with the boiling vinegar and seal immediately. This will be a spicy and sour pickle.

TINY SWEET PICKLES
so good for chicken or tuna sandwiches

8 quarts small cucumbers
1 cup salt (not iodized)
1 gallon water (for soaking)
1 quart water (additional)
 2 quarts vinegar
1½ cups sugar
1 Tbsp. each: allspice, cloves
          cinnamon

Soak the cucumbers in strong salt water overnight, drain and rinse them. In a large kettle, heat the additional water, vinegar, sugar, and spices tied in a bag to the boiling point. Drop the cucumbers into the boiling vinegar. Boiling with stop, so let the mixture come to a good rolling boil, then pack quickly the pickles into sterilized jars and pour the hot liquid over them. Seal lightly.

The secret of making crisp, crunchy pickles is to see that they come just to the boiling point after they are added to the hot liquid. Do not let them continue to boil.

Diane Messenger of Bellevue, Michigan, shared this recipe with me. She says you'll never make any other kind of pickles. Pumpkin makes an interesting sweet pickle. It is especially good with pork and poultry dishes or as a garnish to fruit salad.

PICKLED PUMPKIN

5-6 lbs. pumpkin (pared)
1 pint cider vinegar
3 lbs. sugar
1 tsp. whole cloves
1 Tbsp. cinnamon stick (broken)
2 pieces crystalized ginger

Cut the pumpkin into 1" cubes. Bring the vinegar and sugar to a boil and simmer until the sugar is dissolved. Place the cloves, cinnamon and ginger in a bag. Add to the syrup and boil 5 minutes. Add the pumpkin and bring the mixture back to a fast rolling boil. Boil over low heat exactly 25 minutes, stirring often. Remove the spice bag. Place the pumpkin in sterilized jars, pour the vinegar syrup on top to completely cover and seal. This recipes yields 5 to 6 pints of pickles.

This recipe was very popular during The Depression. We used lots of ½ gallon jars. We used the larger jars for fruit. The quart jars were too small for the popular fruit dumplings when the Aunts and Uncles with 5 or 6 children would come to see us.

DILL PICKLES

Wash and pack medium-sized cucumbers into sterilized half gallon jars, after first placing in the bottom of each jar:

2 heads of dill
4 cloves garlic (to taste)
1 fresh grape leaf (This will help
        preserve the green color.)
1 small red pepper (From a
        bottle of pepper sauce)
a pinch of powdered alum
or
3 or 4 hard unripened grapes

Heat the following to the boiling point and use it to fill the jars to the neck:

1 quart vinegar
1 cup salt (not iodized)
6 quarts water

Seal with good rubbers and lids.

MRS. MILLS' YELLOW TOMATO PRESERVES

1 lbs. small green tomatoes
2 lemons
1 Tbsp. ginger root
1 Tbsp. whole mace
3½ lbs. sugar

Wash tomatoes and prick each one with a fork. Add sugar, 1 lemon sliced thinly and juice of 1 lemon. Mix. Tie mace and ginger root in a thin cloth bag. Add to tomatoes. Heat slowly and simmer gently until fruit is transparent. Remove tomatoes. Boil syrup until thick. Add tomatoes and heat to boiling.

MRS. MILLS' SUN PRESERVES
(cherries or strawberries)

Prepare fruit (cherries or strawberries). Heat slowly to boiling. Stir frquently. Boil slowlly for 8 minutes. Let stand overnight. Pour into shallow dishes or pans. Cover with glass. Set in hot sun for several days or ulntil jice has thickened, and fruit is plump. The juice of 1 lemon may be added to each 2 lbs. of fruit, if desired.

KITCHEN KAPERS: When cooking preserves, cook in oven. You'll have to stir very little, and they cook more quickly because there's heat on all sides.

MEMORIES

PIONEERS

I don't know when our early settlers were first called pioneers. I suspect there will always be pioneers - pioneers in aviation, in the Space Age and computers. But there will never be the resilience, perserverance, and the strength of the '89'ers, the people who made the land runs of Okahoma and The Indian Territory in 1889.

They came with all their earthly goods in 1 wagon, and the milk cow was lead behind the wagon. Included in the wagon were the pots and pans they just had to have and probably wooden boxes to hold their quilts and clothes that doubled for chairs in their temporary homes. There had to be a small stove for cooking and heating. The few farm implements had to have priority. There had to be some groceries like flour, lard, middlin', potatoes, and home canned fruit - enough to last a few weeks. The closest town would be 15-20 miles away; a long day's journey both ways. I bet there was enough vinegar and sugar to make a vinegar cobbler, occasionally, and of course, there had to be molasses.

Maybe there was a hill where they could dig out and build a temporary home - the half dugout with dirt floors. Those dirt floors had rag rugs that were made fromthe best part of shirt tails, dress skirts, and the worn out winter underwear that everybody wore.

The Pioneers were compelled to use cow chips for fuel in the prarie country. Buffalo chips were also usually in good supply. The task of gathering the chips was left to the women and children. When gathering the chips, the mother wore a big apron made from a gunny sack. The children were always nagged to wash their hands. My parents never had to resort to using chips, since we had plenty of mesquite wood. The secret of burning the wood was waiting until it was really dry.

Dugout

I remember saving rags so my grandmother could teach us to make these rugs when she came to see us. The rags were torn ino 1½ strips, sewn together and rolled into balls. They were either braided, sewn into the desired shape or crocheted. My grandmother preferred to crochet them. When we didn't have the proper hook, my father went to the creek bottom, got a piece of boidarc wood and whittled her out a needle. I still have that needle, but the hook has been broken off.

OUR CLOTHES

Our clothes, looking back now, were beautiful. My mother could design by looking at the dresses in the Sears and Roebuck catalog. She only had basic patterns, like the sleeves and the armholes; and she could handle the rest. For trim the dressess were smocked, tucked, hand hemstitched with lace on the edge of the hemstitching, and embroidered with silk thread. Our Sunday dresses for Summer were made from pongee, voile or silk crepe de chene. The Winter ones were made of wool. The pongee was smocked. My father and brother had a pongee dress shirt for Sunday.

I remember finding a $1 bill in Mineral Wells. It was enough money to buy voile to make 2 dresses. They were embroidered in blue silk thread and blue ribbon streamers. That dollar also bought rayon knee length socks with the prettiest cuffs to match the dresses. None of our cousins had anything as pretty, unless my mother made them. She sat up lots of nights until midnight sewing, so we could have new dresses for Sunday. She sewed with the kerosene lamp sitting on the sewing machine. Her button holes were a piece of art, in other words, they didn't look like "hogeyes."

QUILTS AND BEDDING

In the Winter the neighbors would meet to quilt. Sometimes my father would help my mother tack quilts. That was when she covered the worn ones with Cretone. They were so pretty - a very bright floral pattern.

Everyone had a quilt box. It was made from one by twelves. It had a ruffle around 3 sides, and the hinged lid was padded and doubled for a seat, like a window box. It was so pretty covered with that pretty Cretone.

All the quilts had protectors made from tails of shirts and good parts of dresses. They were about 14 inches wide and the length of the quilt. It was folded in the center, sewed on the front side and then sewed to the wrong side. This helped keep the quilt clean, and they lasted longer.

For bed spreads we had embroidered sheets. The design was usually a big basket in the center. Then my mother would crochet lace about 2 to 3 inches wide to go on 3 sides. Marie and I embroidered the pillow cases. We usually used unbleached muslin, often called *brown domestic*. It was cheaper. Now, the unbleached muslin is more popular. We usually made our own patterns. They were traced off with carbon paper until it was completely worn out. We often put a piece of paper over a piece of embroidery, rub it with an aluminum spoon or cup. Then we would have the pattern we wanted.

YESTERDAY'S KITCHEN

There was a shelf on the back porch that held our wash pan and water bucket made of gray enamel. The dipper stayed in the water bucket. We didn't use a gourd for a dipper, but many people did. The water shelf was moved in the house behind the stove during the Winter. Even in the house, there would be ice in the bucket during the coldest months.

Every kitchen had an eating table and a work table. The eating table had an oilcloth tablecloth. It was left on the table all the time; you just wiped off the table with the dishcloth (rag). My mother scalloped the edge and stitched the scallops with black embroidery thread. The oilcloth was ordered from the Sears and Roebuck catalog. The viddles, as leftovers were called, were left on the eating table and covered with a white cloth that was usually made from the best part of a worn out sheet. This food was used used for "supper" (evening meal). Some kitchens had a pie safe (just called safe) that held the leftovers instead of leaving the food on the eating table covered with a cloth.

There were no built-in cabinets, but every kitchen had a store-bought cabinet; the most desired one was a Hoosier. It was so complete. When the door opened there was a place for the bread board. The bread board made a shelf that held the wooden bowl that the biscuits, teacakes and pie crust were mixed in. On the other side there was a drawer for the cuptowels, a metal lined drawer for the bread and 2 other drawers. In the center was a divided drawer for the knifes and forks (not silverware). The spoons were put in a spoon holder and set on the eating table. In the middle section there was a bin that sifted out the flour with a crank, and a canister that held meal and sugar. In the side of the bottom was a door that held lids for the pots and pans. The top space held the dishes. For the working space there was a porcelain tabletop that pulled out the make a bigger working space.

A good example of a Hoosier cabinet is in the cover photograph of this cookbook. It's from the kitchen of Ilena Vernon of Altus, Oklahoma.

THE WATER COOLER

Most of us now living can't imagine what it was like to live without a electric refrigerator. We didn't have electricity in rural areas until World War II. Even if you lived in town, the wooden iceboxes came first. The iceman came in your house with a block of ice on his back if you had an icebox and put your card in the window. That card told him what size of block you wanted. He wore a rubber protector across his back to keep him dry. The ice block was placed on 1 side of the icebox, and the food on the other side. The food didn't keep anyway like now, but it was an improvement. You had to put a pan under the icebox to catch the drippings. If you forgot to empty it before you went to bed, you were in trouble. I heard how 1 person handled that situation. She had a hole bored into the floor under the icebox and fitted an aluminum funnel into a ¾" pipe that lead through the foundation to the side of the house. Then she planted mint at the edge of the drip. Really clever I would say. The first icewagons were horsedrawn. Sometimes, the iceman might drop some ice pieces; there were always some kids around to pick them up.

After the wooden boxes came metal ones with a finish similar to the refrigerators of today. Their brand name was *Coolerator*. They were better insulated and kept the food better. By this time, the iceman had a motor vehicle and delivered in the country. When we live in the country, eighteen miles from town, we would buy ice on Saturday if we went to town. We'd wrap it in paper and then an old quilt to bring it home. We didn't try to preserve food with it; we used it for some ice drinks and to cool us off.

Then after the Coolerator came the electric refrigerator. We couldn't afford an icebox when I lived at home, but we soon bought an electric refrigerator after I married. As I remember, the payments were less than 2 dollars a month and about 5 dollars down. I think with interest and all the cost was about 90 dollars. It was the greatest invention since slice bread. Incidently, one of the most popular bridal gifts was a bread board and knife.

With a new refrigerator, we began making frozen desserts, like ice cream in a refrigerator ice tray. When made in ice trays, we used evaporated milk or whipping cream and took it out of the trays when partially frozen and stirred. Then the mixture was put back in the tray to finish freezing. These frozen desserts were used a lot during World War II. Fruit, either fresh or canned, was usually available. You could substitute syrup for sugar when sugar was rationed during the War. I still make ice cream in the refrigerator, occasionally, and it is still just as good.

MOVING TO OKLAHOMA

The full school year before we moved to Oklahoma, Mother, Marie and I lived in a duplex in Mineral Wells, Texas (18 miles away), to go to school. My brother was not at home by this time to drive the buggy to school. My father stayed on the farm and picked us up on Friday afternoon and brought us back in time for school Monday morning. The next school year we stayed with Aunt Lela Bonds and Grandpa Bonds. We had kitchen priviledges, fixed our breakfast and lunch; and this time we had a paper sack. My mother would make us those Old Timey Tea Cakes.

By the first of January my father sold the farm, and we moved to Blair, Oklahoma. We thought it was a good move. For the first time we could walk to school just a few blocks away, and we could walk home for dinner (lunch). My mother had learned the millinery trade and put in a millinery and dress shop. My father was running a gas station and sold tires, tubes and other accessories. We had only lived in Oklahoma for 6 months when my mother was killed in a tornado. She was 35 years old. Marie was eleven, and I was thirteen.

My father was working in a grocery store when the *Depression* hit. In the meantime, he had a nervous break-down. This was 3 years into *The Depression;* sometimes there was no income. He swapped a cow for a truck, and he and my brother started a little produce business. Due to the stress and breakdown, my father couldn't make change or drive. But after they started this new business, my father's health began to improve. My parents were both brilliant; they were just born in a era where it was hard to succeed - no matter how hard one tried. Those people born in this era were victims of circumstances under which they had no control.

My father did manage to keep us in school, and we finished high school with high honors. Marie and I were in the same grade due to birthdays and convenience. I was only 15 months older than her. There was no way we could go to college - no scholarships, student loans or grants. My aunt told us she could find us a place to stay for our room and board if we could manage the rest. That, too, was impossible.

In June of the next year, I married Marvin Allen and moved 10 miles away to Altus, Oklahoma, where I still live. Marvin owned a very crude barber and beauty shop when we married. Marie came to live with us, and we both went to work in the beauty shop. It was in *The Great Depression*. I did permanents for laundry, quilt tops, quilting, canned fruit, dressmaking, fresh produce; anything we could use that would replace money. Marvin and I operated our beauty shop for over 50 years.

My sister married the young man she was dating when I married. He was a farmer; they worked hard, managed well and became very prosperous. He died suddenly of a heart attack in 1977. Marie still lives in the same town, and we talk or see each other every day.

These hard times did not leave us bitter; it just made us stronger.

Marvin and Thelma
in the eary years of their marriage

WORLD WAR II DAYS

I doubt if there is a person living when Pearl Harbor was bombed that doesn't remember exactly what he was doing. Marvin and I had been to church, eaten the noon meal and had driven 10 miles to help celebrate my grandmother's birthday which was December 7, 1861. My father met us at the door; I could tell by the look on his face that there was something the matter before he spoke a word. He said, "We're in war! The Japs have bombed Pearl Harbor, and the President is calling a joint session of Congress and will declare war in the morning." Everyone hovered around the radio to hear war declared by President Roosevelt. It left you with a really sad feeling.

Everybody's life changed from that day on. We were found totally unprepared, but everybody pitched in and did their part. Many went to work in defense plants. Ships, tanks and all the other things had to be manufactured that were needed to win the war. Women who were used to having maids do their work started doing their work, including laundry. They ran the family businesses while their husbands were working for Uncle Sam. There was a labor shortage in every class of work. Really, The Depression didn't end until World War II. Every woman that had a Teachers Cerificate began to teach. My aunt returned to the classroom. With the help of her husband, who was too old for the draft, she prepared her high school math for the next day. She not only taught math, she coached the dramatic plays, taught glee club, coached basketball, and anything else there was to do. Nobody complained of the long hours or poor pay; we just did what had to be done. School turned out at noon for the kids to pull cotton boles. The mothers and teachers joined them.

My son-in-law who was born in 1946 asked me what stood out the most in my mind about The War. I didn't have to think long for the answer. It was seeing young men everywhere you looked and a few women in uniforms - just kids. You saw them when you went to the Post Office, the bank and the grocery. You saw them at the bus and train stations. Sweethearts, mothers, fathers, wives, little sisters, big sisters, little brothers, big brothers. You were either meeting them or saying "goodbye." No matter the circumstances; it was sad. My son-in-law was really surprised when I didn't say that rationing wasn't the hardest. That was the easiest part. The Depression Days had prepared us for that. We usually found ways to "use it up - wear it out, make it do or do without."

Rationing became real and real soon. World War I taught us the need for that. Silk hose went to $10.00 a pair. At the time of World War II we had gone to nylon hose. There were no nylons; it was needed for pararchutes and other war purposes. Hose were made from cotton. The manufacturers did a good job, but cotton hose didn't compare to nylon. Women, after the war was over, if they heard of a store that had nylons would drive 30-40 miles for nylons only to hear they were sold out.

Everything was scarce, hard to get or rationed. Shoes, tires, gas, household applicances, food, coffee, and sugar; things you never dreamed of were rationed. Gas was rationed not to save gas, but to save rubber. The public never really understood that. The shortage of fabric was overcome by making suits with only 1 pair of trousers, no cuffs and narrow labels. OPA (Office of Price Control Administration) decreed that women's skirts be ½" above the knee. Patched clothing became the latest fashion. People in small towns walked to work. It was the patriotic thing to do. Car pooling was practiced.

My brother-in-law, a farmer, needed a new fence - no material. So he patched and patched the old fence. This was hard on overalls, and there was a shortage; so my sister patched and patched, becoming a patch artist. When my brother-in-law was issued new tires to farm with, he hid them under the bed being afraid to put them in a conspicuous place.

Everybody that had the least bit of space planted a Victory Garden. It was estimated that at least ⅓ of the vegetables eaten in 1943 were grown in Victory Gardens.

Probably no other government agency affected more lives than the OPA or received more criticism; but the necessity of its work was understood. It not only saved taxpayers billions of dollars in cost of war and prevented suffering and chaos. Price control was on just about everything, including rent. In the end we came out in better shape than after World War I.

There were 5 ration books, but only 4 were used. The fifth book was already printed when Japan surrendered. The production of the Ration Book No. 4 was the largest printing job in history. That job required 18 printing plants scattered all over the country, 96 carloads (train) of special paper to halt counterfeiting, 7,500 gallons of paste to fasten pages (saving seventy five tons of wire stapling enough to make 1,500 Garland rifles), 87,000 pounds of ink, 750,000 boxes, 4 freight trains of 30 cars each to haul the boxes to over 7,000 ration boards.

The general conversation when you met somebody, especially if you hadn't seen them lately, was where is "John," when did you hear from him last or when will he have a furlough? We ate out most of the time, because we worked such long hours. We had more sugar than we needed, so I saw that every serviceman I knew about had sugar for his favorite dessert when home on furlough.

I suppose the question asked the most was "when will it ever be over?" War bonds were purchased. Movie stars sold war bonds and went to the training camps to entertain. Kate Smith gave all the proceeds from "God Bless America" to the war effort. We can well remember VJ Day (Victory In Japan). Everything stopped, and businesses closed. Every siren in town blew full blast. What a welcome sound. We had won the war! What a price to pay, not in material things; they can be replaced. But we can't buy more boys and girls. Freedom does not come cheap.

This photograph from World War II shows my husband's nephew, Jack Allen (3rd from left, front row), and his B - 1 7 crew. Jack was a waist gunner and was shot down at Keal, Denmark. He was captured and made a prisoner of war for 17 months. When they were caught, they marched 200 miles to Krms, Austria, to the famous prison camp Stalag 17. It was on this march they nearly starved to death. Even the guards didn't have food either. Women along the road fed them when they had food. They caught chickens and cooked them. Nobody cared; everyone was just trying to survive. In the camp they ate soup made from potato peelings.

Life at the prison camp was made into the Academy Award winning movie, "Stalag 17." Jack said the movie was very authentic.

World War II, by necessity, made creative cooks. We learned the make our sugar ration book go farther by doing lots of substituting, dark syrup for brown sugar, white syrup for white sugar, and just about everything that called for sugar. Sometimes, we omitted sugar by using fruit - chopped prunes, raisins, applesauce. Spices were increased in the recipes. Syrup was especially good in cobblers and frozen desserts.

Taken from a farm club cookbook, dated in 1946-47.

SUGARLESS BROWNIES

½ cup shortening
1 cup dark corn syrup
4 Tbsp. cocoa
¾ cup sifted flour
½ tsp. baking powder
¼ tsp. salt
2 well-beaten eggs
¾ cup nuts
½ tsp. vanilla

Cream shortening until fluffy. Add sugar and beat. Add cocao and beaten eggs and mix well. Add dry ingredients and add to creamed mixture. Add vanilla and nuts. Bake in shallow pan for 350° fo9r about 20 minutes. Don't overcook.

INDEX

PORK

POULTRY

BEEF

DESSERTS

COOKIES AND CANDIES

BREADS

SALADS AND SOUPS

RELISHES AND PRESERVES

MEMORIES

THELMA ALLEN PERSONAL APPEARANCES

When her schedule permits, Thelma Allen would like to talk to your group about the writing of her cookbooks, her memories and how-to-start a new business in your retirement years.

Mrs. Allen is available for special appearances at your:

Church group
Social club
Civic organization
In-store promotion
Radio and television talk show
Business

FUND RAISING PROGRAM

The "Recipes From Sweet Yesterday" cookbooks are excellent products that can be sold by your group for your fund raising needs.

FOR APPEARANCE AVAILABILITY
AND INFORMATION
ON OUR FUND RAISING PROGRAM,
CONTACT:

Michael Allen
Michael Allen Entertainment
P, O. Box 111510
Nashville, TN 37222

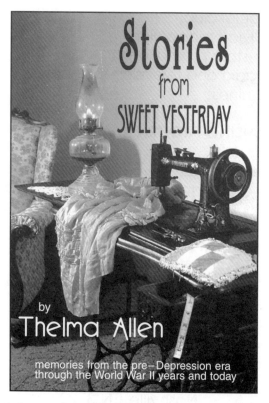

Visit *our website*

at

www.sweetyesterday.com

- Free Recipes

- Product News & Updates

- Thelma Allen Personal Appearances

- Latest News From Sweet Yesterday

Thanks

for purchasing the
Recipes From Sweet Yesterday
cookbooks.

We know you will enjoy your books.
**You may want to purchase some more copies
for *gifts for friends and relatives!***

Here's a *checklist* for you to use.
Write volume number by name.

☐ Birthday gifts for: Date needed:

(name)_____   _____

(name)_____   _____

(name)_____   _____

☐ Wedding gifts for:

(name)_____   _____

(name)_____   _____

(name)_____   _____

☐ Christmas gifts for:

(name)_____   _____

(name)_____   _____

(name)_____   _____

☐ Graduation gifts for:

(name)_____   _____

(name)_____   _____

(name)_____   _____

☐ Mother's Day gifts for:

(name)_____   _____

(name)_____   _____

(name)_____   _____

ORDER EXTRA COPIES
of the
"SWEET YESTERDAY" COOKBOOKS
and the
"STORIES FROM SWEET YESTERDAY"
CASSETTE

NO. OF COPIES___**VOLUME 1** @ $10.^{00} each
NO. OF COPIES___**VOLUME 2** @ $10.^{00} each
NO. OF COPIES___**VOLUME 3** @ $10.^{00} each
NO. OF COPIES___**CASSETTE** @ $10.^{00} each

SUBTOTAL_____

Add 8.25% sales tax (Tenn. residents only)_____
Postage and handling for 1st book - $3^{75}_____
   P & H for each additional book - $1^{25}_____

TOTAL_____

ORDERED BY _____

STREET/APT. NO._____

CITY/STATE/ZIP_____

PHONE (____)_____
We would like to send you product updates by email.
Your email address:_____   ___@_____

MAKE YOUR CHECK OR MONEY ORDER TO: SWEET YESTERDAY.

PLEASE MAIL THIS ORDER FORM WITH YOUR PAYMENT TO:

Sweet Yesterday
P.O. Box 111510
Nashville, TN 37222

Please allow 2 weeks for delivery and always on time
for special occasions. All prices are subject to change
without notice.

ORDER EXTRA COPIES
of the
"SWEET YESTERDAY" COOKBOOKS
and the
"STORIES FROM SWEET YESTERDAY"
CASSETTE

NO. OF COPIES___**VOLUME 1** @ $10.⁰⁰ each
NO. OF COPIES___**VOLUME 2** @ $10.⁰⁰ each
NO. OF COPIES___**VOLUME 3** @ $10.⁰⁰ each
NO. OF COPIES___**CASSETTE** @ $10.⁰⁰ each

SUBTOTAL_____

Add 8.25% sales tax (Tenn. residents only)_____
Postage and handling for 1st book - $3⁷⁵_____
   P & H for each additional book - $1²⁵_____

TOTAL_____

ORDERED BY_____

STREET/APT. NO._____

CITY/STATE/ZIP_____

PHONE (____)_____
We would like to send you product updates by email.
Your email address:_____@_____

MAKE YOUR CHECK OR MONEY ORDER TO: SWEET YESTERDAY.

PLEASE MAIL THIS ORDER FORM WITH YOUR PAYMENT TO:

Sweet Yesterday
P.O. Box 111510
Nashville, TN 37222

Please allow 2 weeks for delivery and always on time
for special occasions. All prices are subject to change
without notice.